AFTER THE REVOLUTION

How to Order:

Single copies may be ordered from Prima Publishing, P.O. Box 1260BK, Rocklin, CA 95677; telephone (916) 632-4400. Quantity discounts are also available. On your letterhead, include information concerning the intended use of the books and the number of books you wish to purchase.

AFTER THE REVOLUTION

A Citizen's Guide to the First Republican Congress in 40 Years

James W. Robinson
with
Russ Colliau

Foreword by Senator Bob Dole

PRIMA PUBLISHING

Production by Steven K. Martin
Interior design and layout by Marian Hartsough
Cover design by Harbison & Solorzano

CIP data available
ISBN 0-7615-0072-3

95 96 97 98 99 CWO 10 9 8 7 6 5 4 3 2 1
Printed in the United States of America

CONTENTS

ACKNOWLEDGMENTS

Russ Colliau has been the best researcher an author could hope to have, which is why I wanted his name on the cover along with mine. It was truly a collaborative effort.

I also wish to thank Ben Dominitz, Jennifer Basye Sander, and Steven Martin of Prima Publishing for the commitment, hard work, and tremendous creativity they devoted to this book.

Thanks also to Senator Bob Dole, Clarkson Hine of the senator's staff, Brian Lungren, Michael McClelland, and Jennifer Evans.

Two individuals who have offered me valuable lessons applicable to both life and politics—especially fighting for what you believe in and maintaining the courage of your convictions even when yours is a lonely voice, and never giving up on your dreams: Dick Lesher and Tom Donohue.

Finally, I have had the rare privilege of working for a total of 12 years for two outstanding national leaders, men of intelligence and integrity, whose dedication to the principles that triumphed on November 8, 1994, is unsurpassed. This book is dedicated to former California Governor George Deukmejian and California Attorney General Dan Lungren.

Foreword

by
Senate Majority Leader
Bob Dole

Most Americans weren't around the last time the Republicans controlled both houses of Congress. I was. It only lasted two years.

If Republicans want to do better this time, then we have to produce. We have to deliver. That is what we intend to do.

I believe the American people elected us to put an end to excessive taxation, spending, and regulation. They elected us to restore America's stature in a world that is still dangerous. Republicans are going to deliver on this agenda not simply because it is good politics but because it is good for America.

The citizens who elected this new Republican Congress will be watching us closely. I welcome that. Applaud us when we do well. Criticize us when we fall short. *After the Revolution: A Citizen's Guide to the First Republican Congress in 40 Years* will help you learn more about us and measure our performance alongside our promises.

I come from a small town in the heartland of middle America. I grew up in an America that offered boundless opportunity, but in return asked for personal responsibility and sacrifice in order to preserve freedom and make possible that opportunity.

With your help, we can restore the promise of America for every citizen. The journey we now begin in this historic new Congress won't be quick or easy, but it is a journey we must make together.

CHAPTER ONE

NOVEMBER 8, 1994:
"The French Revolution ... Without the Guillotine"

When Ronald Reagan swamped Jimmy Carter in the election of 1980, carrying a Republican Senate into office with him, both the incumbent president and the First Lady explained the loss as "a protest vote," not an ideological mandate. When President Reagan won a resounding reelection landslide in 1984, most pundits said it was little more than a function of the genial, optimistic personality of the president, not an endorsement of his conservative agenda. Americans liked Ronald Reagan, we were told, but they didn't like Reaganism.

The story continues. George Bush won in 1988 because he offered a mid-course correction from the right to the center. In 1992, it was the Republicans' turn to explain away an electoral disaster. Americans didn't really want to hire Bill Clinton, many of them suggested. They simply wanted to *fire* George Bush.

November 8, 1994, was different. The message was loud, clear, and indisputable. Whether they loved or hated the result, few observers tried to explain it away as a protest, an aberration, or a backlash against incumbents. After all, not one incumbent Republican representative, senator, or governor lost anywhere in the nation. Yet the Democrats lost 53 seats in the House of Representatives, 9 seats in the Senate, and 11 governorships. Liberal icons such as New York Governor Mario Cuomo and House Speaker Tom Foley were tossed out. A relatively popular Democrat such as Texas Governor Ann Richards was defeated, while a Republican such as California Governor Pete Wilson, down in the polls for most of his term, cruised to a landslide reelection victory.

When it was all over, Republicans had seized control of both houses of Congress for the first time in 40 years and controlled a majority of state houses for the first time since 1970.

In the words of Tom Donohue, president and chief executive officer of the American Trucking Associations, the November 8, 1994, election "was like the French Revolution . . . without the guillotine." To many Democrats, the guillotine would have been less painful.

DEMOCRATS ASK: WHY US? WHY NOW?

What happened? Why did it happen? Why did it happen now? How long will it last? These are the questions being pondered by Washington insiders and media talking heads. As you listen to the pundits predict and prognosticate, just remember: how many of them forecasted what would happen on November 8, 1994?

In fairness, on the surface, 1994 did not appear to be a year of substantial realignment in American politics. Sure, President Clinton was down in the polls, but so were Presidents Nixon and Reagan at the half-way points in their first terms—and no major political disasters visited them in the midterm elections.

Historically, the party in charge of the White House loses Congressional seats two years into its tenure; even more seats in the sixth year of a president's reign. Everyone expected losses for the Democrats this time, but nothing beyond the historical norm. With no major economic crisis or international calamity, there was simply no reason to anticipate a political earthquake.

Even the much ballyhooed anti-incumbent fever failed to excite or forewarn most of the insiders. For years, election cycles seemed to follow a set pattern: in the months leading up to the election the press and pollsters would discern a nasty strain of public antagonism toward incumbent politicians. Predictions of a major housecleaning would follow. Then the votes were counted, and 95–99 percent of incumbent members of Congress were on their way back to Washington, D.C. The public's bark seemed far worse than its bite. But not in 1994.

No single factor explains what happened. Voter anger was apparent two years ago, perhaps planting some of the seeds that flowered into voter revolution in 1994. An incumbent president, George Bush, was turned out of office with the lowest percentage of the vote for a sitting president in nearly 80 years. Nineteen percent of the American electorate cast its vote for an iconoclastic billionaire businessman with a short temper and no governmental experience.

Al From, president of the centrist Democratic Leadership Council, explains the Democrats' loss this way: "Part of it was the president. Part of it was the Congress. Part of it was Washington. The people said, 'we don't like politics as usual. The Democrats are in charge. We're going to make them pay.'"

The culpability of President Clinton in the Democrats' election debacle has been much debated by analysts of all political stripes. Indeed, more than one White House watcher has described the post-election president as appearing visibly depressed. The conventional wisdom among Clinton bashers is that he doesn't stand for anything and doesn't know what he's doing. Thus he can be defeated by derision: Turn him out of office by turning him into another Jimmy Carter—the butt of a big national joke.

Putting aside the fact that a derided and discredited commander-in-chief is bad for America, I disagree with that characterization of President Clinton. I believe the president knows precisely what he stands for and what he wants to accomplish—a liberal agenda that envisions a society defined by an activist and ever-expanding central government. Yet, not wanting to tilt hopelessly at windmills his whole life, President Clinton made a crucial calculation years ago—that to have any hope for a chance to implement his out-of-fashion beliefs, he first had to redefine them, recharacterize them, and repackage them. Should he allow either himself or his ideas to be labeled in the traditional manner, he would be finished.

Until 1994, Clinton's strategy worked astoundingly well. He transformed himself from a bearded, long-haired antiwar protester and McGovern campaign worker into one of the most successful and durable politicians from a conservative, southern state. As a staff member for another governor, I watched Clinton rise to leadership among all the governors through sheer hard work, intelligence, and tenacity, winning the respect of both Democratic and Republican governors. And when he got himself elected President of the United States, he did it in a year in which more substantial Democrats lost their nerve even to run.

Yet two years into a presidency with an arguably lengthy list of legislative achievements, Bill Clinton experienced the worst political humiliation visited upon any president since Richard Nixon. Why?

The reason is not because he believed in nothing, but because he believed in something too much. That something was health care. It was his health-care proposal that unmasked Bill Clinton in the eyes of much of the American public. All the careful calculation, all the years of slipping and sliding away from being tagged as a traditional big-government, tax-and-spend liberal, were demolished by his passionate and sincere embrace of a government takeover of the nation's health-care system, amounting to one-sixth of the entire American economy.

President and Mrs. Clinton's health-care plan unwittingly enabled the American electorate to pull off their blindfolds and pin the tail on the donkey! Clinton and his fellow Democrats—not all incumbents—were identified as the enemy. Rep. Newt Gingrich and the Republicans were seen as the camp offering a positive vision for change.

THE REVOLUTION IN POLITICAL COMMUNICATION

> America our nation has been beaten by
> strangers who have turned our language inside
> out, who have taken the clean words our
> fathers spoke and made them slimy and foul.
>
> —John Dos Passos,
> "Camera Eye 50," *The Big Money*

In an earlier year and from a different perspective, John Dos Passos wrote passionately about the importance of language and communication in a democracy. Corrupt the language and you corrupt the civilization. Control the definitions and the terms of the debate and the dialogue, and you will control the nation's agenda.

As much as they set out to make a revolution in terms of winning a numerical majority in Congress, Newt Gingrich and a close-knit band of like-minded Republicans have for years dreamed of revolutionizing the terms of the debate, changing definitions, and speaking to the American people in dramatically different ways. In fact, they realized they could not achieve the first without the second. "We have to win the definitional argument about how America works," Newt Gingrich told the Heritage Foundation shortly after the November election. "As long as the Left can define America in their terms, we can't win."

In national policy terms, conservatives watched for years as the governing and media elite appropriated certain words and seemed to turn them inside out. When speaking of the budget, a "cut" came to mean not a real reduction in expenditures from the prior year but simply a reduction in a projected increase. "Fairness" in the eyes of many seemed to really mean unfairness; it became a code word for taking more money from the people who earned it and giving it to the people who didn't. "Equal opportunity" seemed to be more about granting *unequal* preferences to some on the basis of special characteristics than it was about stamping out the last vestiges of racism and achieving a society based truly on merit rather than prejudice. The whole concept of "political correctness," which puts off-limits the expression of out-of-the-mainstream terms and ideas, was seen by many conservatives as a manipulation of the national dialogue and in many circumstances a frontal assault on the First Amendment.

Yet in charting the course of the Republican takeover, Gingrich and his allies not only understood the importance of changing the terms and definitions of the political and policy debate, they knew they had to change the venue of the debate as well. If they relied on the established media and the traditional methods of transmitted political messages, they would lose. And so, in the 1994 election cycle, they nurtured and used with great effectiveness alternative outlets of communication—outlets that they are convinced will soon become the dominant ones.

Consider these developments:

- To develop a stable of well-trained, aggressive GOP Congressional candidates around the country as well as to fill the heads of millions of supporters with new ideas, Gingrich and his political operation sent out 700,000 videotapes annually for the last five years.

- A conservative cable TV network called National Empowerment Television carried programs produced by Gingrich and other conservatives into the homes of millions.

- Conservative radio talk-show hosts, led by Rush Limbaugh, connect tens of millions of Americans through phones, radios, and computers in a kind of perpetual national town-hall meeting running all hours of the day and night.

- C-Span, a cable television network featuring gavel-to-gavel coverage of Congress and many other political and governmental events, now reaches 62 million American homes.

Former Republican Congressman Vin Weber was

quoted recently in the *New York Times* as saying this about Gingrich's rise to power and its links to C-Span: "He surely has understood the uses of the media in ways that no Congressional leader has before. A lot of this relates to his concept of nationalizing the election. This was the strategy and using C-Span was part of it—to go directly to the country, talk about what's going on in the Congress, and not permit members to go back to their districts to talk about what they wanted to talk about, like the pork they brought back home."

• Internet, a computer network now linking an estimated 30 million users, as well as other computer networks such as CompuServe, has opened a vast new channel of political communication that completely bypasses the normal channels of network television news and the morning newspaper.

A recent analysis of Gingrich's ascension in the *Los Angeles Times* concluded that a key element was the new Speaker's recognition that a "technological and economic revolution would weaken elite structures, make the economy more international, and make politics more grass-roots."

From national radio talk shows to C-Span and other cable television programming, to millions of Americans exchanging political ideas and electronically conversing with one another about policy through their home computers, political communication has likely been changed by the election of 1994. This election not only produced a profound ideological transformation, it also signified the arrival of a new era in the way language is shaped and transmitted throughout the American community.

BEFORE AND AFTER:
THE SHAPE OF THE NEW CONGRESS

How real is this revolution? Let's look at the numbers.

The Senate

Democrats went into the November 8 election with a 56 to 44 majority. When the votes were tallied, Republicans had picked up eight seats to gain a majority of 52 to 48. Then, to add insult to injury, Democratic Senator Richard Shelby of Alabama switched parties, increasing the new Republican edge to 53 to 47. (Under the Constitution, Vice President Al Gore, a Democrat, still presides as president of the Senate, one of the responsibilities of which is to cast tie-breaking votes.)

Democrats did not pick up a single seat previously held by a Republican. Yet Republicans gained seats previously held by Democrats in the following states:

Arizona—Republican Jon Kyl replaces Democrat Dennis DeConcini, who retired.

Maine—Republican Olympia Snowe replaces Democrat George Mitchell, who retired.

Michigan—Republican Spencer Abraham replaces Democrat Donald Riegle, who retired.

Ohio—Republican Michael DeWine replaces Democrat Howard Metzenbaum, who retired.

Oklahoma—Republican James Inhofe replaces Democrat David Boren, who retired.

Pennsylvania—Republican Rick Santorum defeated incumbent Democrat Harris Wofford.

Tennessee—Republican Bill Frist defeated Democratic incumbent Jim Sasser, and Republican

Fred Thompson defeated Democrat Jim Cooper in an open seat.

Alabama—Republican Richard Shelby replaces Democrat Richard Shelby!

The House of Representatives

Before the November 8 election, Democrats controlled the House of Representatives by a margin of 256 to 178, with one independent. When the votes were counted, Republicans gained 53 seats and now control the House for the first time in 40 years, by a margin of 230 to 204, with one independent.

Not one incumbent Republican representative lost. Former Democratic Speaker Tom Foley not only lost his Speakership, he lost his seat—the first sitting House Speaker to lose in this century.

The All-Important State Houses

The Republicans' electoral sweep was replicated in state houses across the nation. Republicans captured 11 governorships—10 from the Democrats plus Connecticut, where a Republican replaces independent Lowell Weicker—while not losing a single state to the Democrats.

Republicans now control 31 of the 50 governorships, including the mega-states of California, Illinois, Michigan, New York, Ohio, and Texas.

INTERPRETING NOVEMBER 8, 1994: HOW THE PLAYERS PLAYED IT

We took a lickin', a bad lickin'.

—Al From, President,
Democratic Leadership Council

I think it is going to last. This is a revolution the people have wanted for years. They just didn't realize you had to change Congress to do it. As long as we do what we told the American people we would do, it will last.

—Rep. Tom DeLay (R-Texas),
newly elected House Republican whip

I think we want to say to the nation that we have nothing to fear but fear itself. We can dramatically improve the quality of life, the economic opportunity, and the safety of every American between now and the year 2000. . . . We were elected to keep our word and we will keep our word.

—House Speaker Newt Gingrich (R-Georgia)

I accept my share of responsibility in the result of the elections.

—President Bill Clinton

The Grand Old Party, typically affiliated with the status quo, quickly became the party of change. . . . Voters were in an exasperated and surly mood. Plainly, Americans want government to deliver, even if they are not always clear on exactly what they want delivered. Let the new GOP majority be warned: Everything in Tuesday's vote indicates that if voters don't get satisfaction, the electorate will seek more vengeance at the polls two years from now.

—*Los Angeles Times*, November 10, 1994

Republicans have waited a long time for a victory this big. But as George Bush well knows, two years is an eternity in politics. Voters will be watching suspiciously, and two years from now, the Republicans better have more to show for their two years than the Democrats had for the last two.

— *San Jose Mercury News*, November 10, 1994

Even as Republicans strut in victory, Newt Gingrich and his fellow gunslingers of the New Right should be wary: The approval span of the American public is about as long as the interval between clicks of a TV remote control.

The soon-to-be speaker of the House might recall that it was just two short years ago that the New Democrats were boogieing to Fleetwood Mac with visions of Camelot shimmering before their Razorback eyes.

Victory, especially a landslide of the sort Republicans produced last week, is heady stuff. But what's new in American politics begins to look old very fast.

— *San Francisco Examiner*, November 16, 1994

The Democratic Party thought it had received a gift from above when Republicans trotted out their 10-point Contract with America and accompanying pledges to slash committees and committee staffs, audit Congress's books, and otherwise assault business as usual if they took control of Capitol Hill. . . .

The GOP agenda and promise to force votes on it, however, clearly struck a chord with mil-

lions of voters fed up with Congressional gridlock and perks who blame the Democrats who
have held both the executive and legislative
branches the last two years. . . .

Politically, the significance of the Contract
with America is that it caught at just the right
time the public demand to shake up Congress
and made the Democrats seem to be defending
the status quo.

—Jack W. Germond and Jules Witcover,
syndicated columnists, November 13, 1994

It's not good for the country for Bill Clinton to
be so defensive. In a sense, the president
embodies the nation; if he lets himself get
kicked around here, the nation will get kicked
around all over the world.

—William Safire, *New York Times*,
November 17, 1994

Time is the ultimate enemy of all reform, revolution, and even mild change. Sooner or later, the
reformers start liking the perks of office, the
power and the rest. Watch for this, too. Every
time in the last few days that I have heard one of
the victors saying words to the effect that "now
it's our turn" and listened to talk about "payback
time" and turning the tables and so on, I have
thought: this is the most dangerous impulse you
can act on; it will turn you into a variation of
what you profess you are trying to uproot.

—Meg Greenfield, *Newsweek*,
November 21, 1994

The wonder of last week's election is not that the Republicans seized control of Congress. It is that they took so long to do it. The United States has been largely a conservative country since the early 1970s, as shown by its almost unbroken string of Republican presidents. But you wouldn't have known that from the consistent Democratic majorities on Capitol Hill. During the past two decades, Democrats have used seniority, money, and other advantages granted incumbents to create a high seawall against conservative tides that flooded other realms of the political system. Now the public's scorn for experienced leaders, swelled by its disenchantment with Bill Clinton, has torn that wall down. . . .

—Michael R. Beschloss, *Newsweek*,
November 21, 1994

Whither liberalism? Did it die last Tuesday? I don't think so—not if you define liberalism as the belief that government can act to improve the lives to its citizens. There is still a strong public desire for protection from the vicissitudes of age, disease, and economic volatility. The driving force in American politics remains the need to find shelter from The Big Fear: the economic and social uncertainties that have been visited upon the middle class in the global, postmodern era. . . .

The . . . awful thing that happened to liberalism in the 1960s was that public-employee unions were legalized. They are the bureaucracy. They now represent the most powerful

special-interest bloc in the Democratic Party.
Which is why the Democrats are considered, as
the president lamented, "the party of government." The unions are also the single most
powerful force against creativity and competi-
tion in the public sector—and Bill Clinton is
their tribune.

—Joe Klein, *Newsweek*, November 21, 1994

The huge wave about to hit Washington did not
rise suddenly from a flat sea. It is part of a tidal
wave of conservatism that began rising in the
late 1960s because of disappointment with the
Great Society social engineering and dismay
about the coarsening of the culture. This pro-
tracted revolution is actually a restoration, a
reconnection with the most continuous thread
in America's political tradition, commitment to
limited government.

—George Will, *Newsweek*, November 28, 1994

If one thing is clear about the 1990s, it is that
voters will punish incumbents who raise taxes.
In 1990, incumbents of both parties got lower
percentages in House elections than they had
two years before—the only time this has happened in a half a century—after majorities of
both parties colluded in the budget summit tax
hikes. In 1992, George Bush fell 16 points in
four years—almost as much as Lyndon Johnson did during the Vietnam War and Herbert
Hoover did in the Great Depression—after he
broke his "Read my lips, no new taxes"

promise. This year, the Democrats lost eight Senate and 52 House seats—far more than the half-century first-term averages of one Senate and 11 House seats—after they pushed through a tax hike. The message should be clear, even to would-be tax increasers like Office of Management and Budget Director Alice Rivlin: The voters do not want to pay more money for more lousy government.

—Michael Barone, *U.S. News & World Report,*
November 28, 1994

The Democrats were seen—not unreasonably, given their control of the White House and Capitol Hill—as the Establishment and were made to pay. . . .

[They] thought they were the solution, not the problem. They became entranced with the big-picture economic statistics that showed a growing economy, rising employment, low inflation, and a shrinking deficit. What they missed was the undiminished economic anxiety of the large working class. . . .

The Republicans have cast themselves again as enemies of Big Government, and thus as friends of the people.

—*Time,* November 21, 1994

Why did the GOP win? It was the baseball strike, stupid.

—Jamie Malanowski, *New York Times,*
November 17, 1994

CHAPTER TWO

THE REPUBLICAN CONTRACT

What Is It?
What Will It Mean to You?

On September 27, 1994, over 300 Republican candidates for Congress gathered in front of the U.S. Capitol and, one by one, signed a document called the Republican Contract with America.

Democratic experts derided the plan, calling it a return to the "voodoo economics" of the Reagan era. Strategists at the White House were gleeful, thinking they had been handed an opportunity by Republicans to replay their 1992 campaign strategy, which was built on a vilification of the 1980s. President Clinton found new energy on the campaign trail, discarding his standard stump speech, which was a bland recitation of his legislative achievements, and returned to his attack themes of 1992. Talk among the Washington pundits was that Newt Gingrich and the Republican brain trust had been poised to make great electoral gains but threw it all away when they unveiled the Contract.

Even some Republican analysts privately agreed. They winced at giving the Democrats an opportunity to dust off their successful 1992 thematic playbook.

But not California Attorney General Dan Lungren, a current Republican National Committeeman and former member of Congress. "You have to nationalize this election," he told me when the Contract was unveiled. "Incumbent members of Congress have so many advantages in terms of constituent services and local issues, the only way you can turn a sufficient number of them out is to base the campaign on overarching national issues."

Gingrich, Lungren, and other leading members of the Republican brain trust were right. In the words of commentator George Will,

> President Clinton defined the election as a referendum on Ronald Reagan's 1980s, thereby taking up the gauntlet Republicans had thrown down with their Reaganite "contract." The referendum produced a lot of Reagan Republicans. If the election's results had been an indiscriminate massacre of incumbents, the election would have been merely a national temper tantrum. Instead it was a resounding ideological statement.

It is rare that a single document should figure so heavily in any election. Supporters and detractors characterized it many ways, but what exactly does the Contract say? What follows is the official Contract, word for word, as provided by the Republican Party.

CONTRACT WITH AMERICA

As Republican members of the House of Representatives and as citizens seeking to join that body we propose not just to change its policies, but even more important, to restore the bonds of trust between the people and their elected representatives.

That is why, in this era of official evasion and posturing, we offer instead a detailed agenda for national renewal, a written commitment with no fine print.

This year's election offers the chance, after four decades of one-party control, to bring to the House a new majority that will transform the way Congress works. That historic change would be the end of government that is too big, too intrusive, and too easy with the public's money. It can be the beginning of a Congress that respects the values and shares the faith of the American family.

Like Lincoln, our first Republican president, we intend to act "with firmness in the right, as God gives us to see the right." To restore accountability to Congress. To end its cycle of scandal and disgrace. To make us all proud again of the way free people govern themselves.

On the first day of the 104th Congress, the new Republican majority will immediately pass the following major reforms, aimed at restoring the faith and trust of the American people in their government:

✦ First, require all laws that apply to the rest of the country also apply equally to Congress

- ✦ Second, select a major, independent auditing firm to conduct a comprehensive audit of Congress for waste, fraud, or abuse

- ✦ Third, cut the number of House committees and cut committee staff by one-third

- ✦ Fourth, limit the terms of all committee chairs

- ✦ Fifth, ban the casting of proxy votes in committee

- ✦ Sixth, require committee meetings to be open to the public

- ✦ Seventh, require a three-fifths majority vote to pass a tax increase

- ✦ Eighth, guarantee an honest accounting of our federal budget by implementing zero base-line budgeting

Thereafter, within the first 100 days of the 104th Congress, we shall bring to the House floor the following bills, each to be given full and open debate, each to be given a clear and fair vote, and each to be immediately available this day for public inspection and scrutiny.

1. The Fiscal Responsibility Act

A balanced-budget/tax-limitation amendment and a legislative line-item veto to restore fiscal responsibility to an out-of-control Congress, requiring them to live under the same budget constraints as families and business.

2. The Taking Back Our Streets Act

An anti-crime package including stronger truth-in-sentencing, "good faith" exclusionary rule exemptions, effective death penalty provisions, and cuts in social spending from this summer's "crime" bill to fund prisons and additional law enforcement to keep people secure in their neighborhoods and kids safe in their schools.

3. The Personal Responsibility Act

Discourage illegitimacy and teen pregnancy by prohibiting welfare to minor mothers and denying increased AFDC for additional children while on welfare, cut spending for welfare programs, and enact a two-years-and-out provision with work requirements to promote individual responsibility.

4. The Family Reinforcement Act

Child-support enforcement, tax incentives for adoption, strengthening rights of parents in education, stronger child pornography laws, and an elderly dependent-care tax credit to reinforce the central role of families in American society.

5. The American Dream Restoration Act

A $500-per-child tax credit, begin repeal of the marriage tax penalty, and creation of American Dream Savings Accounts to provide middle-class tax relief.

6. The National-Security Restoration Act

No U.S. troops under U.N. command, and restoration of the essential parts of our national-security funding to strengthen our national defense and maintain our credibility around the world.

7. The Senior Citizens Fairness Act

Raise the Social Security earnings limit, which currently forces seniors out of the workforce, repeal the 1993 tax hikes on Social Security benefits, and provide tax incentives for private long-term-care insurance to let older Americans keep more of what they have earned over the years.

8. The Job Creation and Wage Enhancement Act

Small-business incentives, capital-gains tax cut and indexation, neutral cost recovery, risk assessment/cost-benefit analysis, strengthening the Regulatory Flexibility Act, and unfunded mandate reform to create jobs and raise worker wages.

9. The Commonsense Legal Reform Act

"Loser pays" laws, reasonable limits on punitive damages, and reform of product-liability laws to stem the endless tide of litigation.

10. The Citizen Legislature Act

A first-ever vote on term limits to replace career politicians with citizen legislators.

Further, we will instruct the House Budget Committee to report to the floor and we will work to enact additional budget savings, beyond the budget cuts specifically included in the legislation described above, to ensure that the federal budget deficit will be less than it would have been without the enactment of these bills.

Respecting the judgment of our fellow citizens as we seek their mandate for reform, we hereby pledge our names to the Contract with America.

THE FINE PRINT

The Contract with America is brief and to the point. Yet behind each policy goal there is detail, a legislative history, and sharp debate. During the 1994 election campaign, the Republican National Committee shed light on the Contract with America in a campaign document. What follows is the Republicans' policy analysis accompanying their Contract.

◆ ◆ ◆

This written Contract with America promises decisive votes on ten major bills in the first 100 days of the first Republican-controlled House of Representatives in 40 years, and a "checklist" of Congressional reforms that would be enacted on the first day. . . .

Only a signed, written contract can pierce the shell of cynicism encasing so many Americans after nearly two years of broken promises and waffling by the most "spin" addicted administration ever to grace the White House. With the written Contract in hand, the public can hold a Republican majority accountable and if the terms are not met, "throw the rascals out."

The Contract is rooted in three core principles:

❖ **Accountability**

   The federal government is too big and spends too much, and elected officials and unelected bureaucrats have become so entrenched and protected as to be unresponsive to the public they are supposed to serve. We must make government more efficient, make sure the taxpayers get their money's worth, and wrest accountability from special-interest groups and return it to the public. The Contract includes a number of substantive reforms to restore accountability to a government writ larger than ever imagined by our founding fathers.

❖ Responsibility

At the same time this administration defaults on its proper responsibility for national security and mistakes a responsibility to protect the public from violent crime for an opportunity to spend billions more on social programs, myriad government programs usurp personal responsibility from families and individuals and our judicial system saps our nation's productivity and encourages frivolous "get-rich-quick" lawsuits. The Contract seeks to restore a proper balance between government and personal responsibility.

❖ Opportunity

Republicans want to restore the opportunity for all Americans to achieve the American Dream, which now exceeds the grasp of too many families. Burdensome government regulations stifle wages, economic growth levels are frustratingly below the post-World War II norm, and the average family today spends more on taxes than it spends on food, clothing, and shelter combined. The result is that middle-class families are making their first home purchase later in life, scrambling to pay college tuition, and often putting a second earner in the market not to support the household but just to support the cost of government.

The American people have grown leery of the Clinton administration and believe the country is on the wrong track. Simply standing firm against the Democrats' tax-

and-spend-and-regulate agenda is greatly appreciated by today's public, but this Contract goes the extra step of providing a positive policy agenda for putting the nation back on the right track.

The Contract with America is an opportunity to restore the American Dream with creative legislative solutions and at the same time to restore trust between the people and their elected representatives and make us all proud again of the way free people govern themselves.

The Contract represents a dramatic change in direction for federal policy making, and the pace of 10 major bills in the first 100 days indicates the magnitude of change to come.

1. Balanced Budget Amendment/Line-Item Veto (The Fiscal Responsibility Act)

Controlling spending is the primary means to controlling the deficit. Republicans favor institutional reforms that would pressure Congress to cut spending. These reforms, the balanced budget amendment and a real line-item veto, are also extremely popular with the American people. According to a recent *Washington Post*/ABC News poll, more than 75 percent of Americans favored a balanced budget amendment.

Regrettably, the White House and Congressional majority, whose power depends on the ability to deliver huge spending projects, have blocked such institutional reform. Indeed, Democrats in Congress have an overall record of voting for spending bills twice as often as Republicans. The first bill in the House Republicans' Contract with America contains two powerful, commonsense ways to control Congress's penchant for spending:

1.   A balanced budget amendment to the
     Constitution with a tax-limitation provision,

which requires a three-fifths vote by both the House and Senate to raise taxes.

2. In order to regain control over spending, the Fiscal Responsibility Act gives the president a permanent line-item veto. The bill calls for an up-or-down vote on the president's package of rescissions, and the cuts would automatically become effective unless Congress rejects them. If Congress rejects the package the president can veto the rejection, and a two-thirds vote would be required to overturn it.

2. Deterring Crime (The Taking Back Our Streets Act)

There was a time when criminals knew that if they committed a violent crime, they would be punished severely. But during the 1960s and 1970s, liberals—both members of Congress and members of the bench and bar—declared war on swift and certain punishment. The Taking Back Our Streets Act strikes at the heart of our violent crime problem by fixing the problems with the recently passed crime bill and by fixing larger problems that have developed over the past years in our criminal justice system.

❖ An Effective Death Penalty

Tightens loopholes in the federal death penalty by requiring the imposition of the death penalty if the jury finds that aggravating factors outweigh mitigating factors. Without this revision, the federal death penalty is vulnerable to challenge on Eighth Amendment grounds. Also, this bill strictly limits the time for filing appeal petitions in federal courts and gives judges the power to dismiss clearly frivolous cases. This is perhaps the most important reform in establishing a credible death penalty to deter violent crime.

❖ Deterring Gun Crimes

This provision would require a 10-year mandatory minimum sentence for the use of a gun during the commission of a state or federal felony. The penalties increase to 20 years for the second gun crime and life for the third. Although these crimes could still be prosecuted at the state level, the mere threat of serving a 10-year sentence with no parole in federal prison is enough to make violent criminals leave their guns at home.

❖ Mandatory Victim Restitution

For the last 40 years, victims of violent crime have been the forgotten casualties in our surrender to violent crime. The act requires criminals to pay full restitution to victims for damages caused as a result of the crime.

❖ Law Enforcement Block Grants

The crime bill passed by Congress in August contains so many compartmentalized programs for prevention and attaches so many strings to grants to hire police officers that many cities and states have given up on these funds. Republicans propose $10 billion in block grants for the police- and law-enforcement-run crime prevention funds so that local officials, who know local crime problems, can make the decisions on how to use these funds to fight crime.

❖ Truth-in-Sentencing and Real Prisons

The prison provisions of the crime bill can be fixed in three simple steps:

1. **Truth-in-sentencing.** All funds for prison construction made available under the crime bill should be conditioned on states adopting, or making significant progress toward, truth-in-sentencing. This provision alone would go a long way toward keeping violent criminals—who now serve only about one-third of their sentences—in jail for at least 85 percent of their sentences.

2. **Real prisons.** All funds should go to construction of real incarceration facilities, not the "alternatives" to incarceration allowed in the crime bill.

3. **Transfer funds to prisons for violent criminals.** Funding for prisons should be increased to $10.5 billion—the amount the Bureau of Prisons has estimated would cover the costs of incarcerating two-time violent felons for at least 85 percent of their sentences. These funds would be available from funds freed up from the block granting of police and prevention spending, and would not constitute an unfunded mandate.

❖ Legal Technicalities Reform

The so-called exclusionary rule of evidence requires judges to exclude evidence of a defendant's guilt if it was gathered illegally—a legitimate concern. But the exclusionary rule works to exclude evidence of guilt even in cases where the police thought they were acting legally—that is, according to a valid warrant or following proper procedures. This broad application of the rule only gets criminals off on technicalities. The GOP provision creates a good faith exception to the exclusionary rule.

❖ **Stopping Abusive Prisoner Lawsuits**

Today, states are forced to spend millions of dollars to defend prison lawsuits to improve prison conditions. Unfortunately, many of these suits are frivolous, tying up scarce state resources by abusing federal laws and the Constitution. They have also increasingly resulted in federal judges running state prison systems. The Taking Back Our Streets Act would reverse this trend by preventing abuse of the criminal justice system by prisoners, without depriving them of avenues to seek legitimate redress of grievances.

❖ **Streamlining Deportation of Criminal Aliens**

States today spend hundreds of millions of dollars holding illegal aliens convicted of violent crimes. This proposal would allow these aliens to be deported immediately after release from prison.

3. Welfare Reform (The Personal Responsibility Act)

In the mid-1960s, President Lyndon Johnson and the Democrat-controlled Congress launched a War on Poverty with the intended hope of securing a "Great Society." The federal government was motivated to fight poverty through a number of new federal programs and by expanding existing ones, such as Aid to Families with Dependent Children (AFDC). More than 25 years later, Johnson's War on Poverty has been an unqualified failure. Despite spending trillions of dollars, it has had the unintended consequence of making welfare more attractive than work to many families, and once welfare recipients become dependent on public assistance, they are caught in the now-familiar "welfare trap."

The Personal Responsibility Act would change destructive social behavior by enacting a welfare reform plan that attacks illegitimacy, requires work, and saves money.

❖ Ending Dependency on AFDC

States have the option of ending AFDC to families that have been on the welfare rolls for two years, if at least one year has been spent in a work program. All states must terminate AFDC payments to families who have received a total of five years of welfare payments.

❖ Attacking Illegitimacy and Teen Pregnancy

Mothers under 18 would not receive AFDC benefits, and the proposal also gives states the option of prohibiting AFDC and housing benefits to mothers aged 18 to 20. Savings from this provision will be converted into block grants to states for services—but not cash benefits—to these mothers and children. Welfare mothers would no longer receive AFDC benefits for the birth of additional children. Lastly, in order for mothers on welfare to receive AFDC benefits, paternity must be established.

❖ Requiring Work, Not Welfare

By the year 2000, 1.5 million AFDC recipients will be required to work. (Despite all his rhetoric about getting people off welfare, President Clinton's bill requires only about 250,000 AFDC recipients to participate in work programs after five years.) The Republican bill also requires at least one able-bodied parent in a two-parent family to work 32 hours per week in a jobs program.

❖ Cutting Welfare Spending

This welfare plan caps the spending growth of several major welfare programs—AFDC, Supplemental Security Income, and public housing. The cap is adjusted for inflation and poverty population. The plan consolidates 10 nutrition programs, including food stamps, WIC, and the school lunch program, into one discretionary block grant to states. With the exception of emergency Medicaid assistance, welfare benefits are eliminated to noncitizens. Currently, noncitizens qualify for AFDC, SSI, Food Stamps, Medicaid, public housing, and a host of other public-aid programs.

❖ Expanding Flexibility to States

Recognizing that the best welfare solutions come from the states, not Washington, D.C., the Personal Responsibility Act allows states to design their own work programs and determine who participates in the work programs. It also allows states to opt out of the current AFDC program and convert their share of AFDC payments into fixed annual block grants, thus removing federal control over the program.

4. Strong Families and Children (The Family Reinforcement Act)

The family is the core of American society. It is the principal mechanism through which values, knowledge, discipline, and motivation are passed from one generation to the next. But rather than bolstering the American family, the policies of the Clinton administration undermine it. The Family Reinforcement Act strengthens the rights of parents—rejecting the Democratic Party view that "government knows best." The bill includes:

❖ **Strengthened Rights of Parents**

This provision strengthens parents' rights to supervise their children's participation in any federally funded program and to shield their children from federally sponsored surveys that involve intrusive questioning.

❖ **Child-Support Enforcement**

To facilitate interstate enforcement of child-support and visitation orders, states would be required to give "full faith and credit" to such orders issued by the courts or administrative procedures of other states. A uniform abstract of a child-support order, for use by all state courts, will help to streamline and expedite enforcement of such orders. Non-custodial parents with child-support arrearages who seek public assistance will face a work requirement to ensure that they resume payments.

❖ **Tax Incentives for Adoption**

A tax credit to make it easier for families to adopt.

❖ **Strengthen Child Pornography and Sexual Assault Provisions**

Enhances penalties for child pornography and increases sentences for criminal sexual conduct.

❖ **Dependent-Care Tax Credit for Seniors**

This provision aims to keep families intact by providing financial assistance to families who might otherwise have to place parents or grandparents in a nursing home. It provides a $500 dependent-care tax credit for families caring for a dependent elderly parent or grandparent.

5. Family and Middle-Class Tax Cuts (The American Dream Restoration Act)

The president promised middle-class tax relief during the campaign but instead gave families the biggest tax increase in American history—$275 billion over five years, including higher taxes on gasoline and Social Security benefits that added to the tax burden of the middle class.

The average family today spends more on taxes than it spends on food, clothing, and shelter combined. Many families now need a second earner not to support the household, but to support the government. Middle-income families are forced to buy their first homes later in life and must scramble to send their children to college. The American Dream Restoration Act (ADRA) would deliver relief from the heavy burden of government and let families keep more of their hard-earned dollars to pursue their own version of the American Dream. Its provisions include:

❖ **$500-per-Child Tax Credit**

The ADRA includes a $500-per-child tax credit for families with annual incomes up to $200,000. The family tax credit would benefit at least 50 million families, 90 percent of whom earn less than $75,000 a year. For example, the tax credit will cut by more than a third the tax burden for a family of four with a $28,000 annual income, helping to scale back the heavy tax burden the Democrats imposed on the American people last year.

❖ Reform the Anti-Marriage Tax Bias

The 1993 Clinton tax increases and expanded Earned Income Tax Credit resulted in many married couples across the income spectrum paying higher taxes than they would by filing as two singles. For example, two single people who each earn $40,000 pay $6,633 each in taxes. Once married, their tax liability leaps to $14,551, or $1,285 more. This bill would reform the tax code to make it fairer to married couples.

❖ American Dream Savings Accounts

Individual Retirement Accounts (IRAs) were a very popular savings instrument for middle Americans before the 1986 Tax Act severely restricted their use. The American Dream Savings Accounts would greatly expand IRAs to all Americans, allowing contributions of up to $2,000 per year. The return on this investment would not be subject to taxation if the new IRA accounts are used for:

- post-secondary education expenses for IRA holders, their children, or grandchildren

- first-time home purchase

- medical expenses or long-term-care insurance

- retirement

The American Dream Savings Accounts will be "back ended" (contributions will be taxable when made, but eligible withdrawals are tax-free), with an option for current IRA holders to cash out, pay taxes, and move into the new American Dream Accounts.

6. Strengthen Defense
(The National-Security Restoration Act)

President Clinton's 1994 Department of Defense Authorization Bill represented the first part of a defense budget that threatens to erode America's standing abroad and undermine our ability to defend our national interests. It guts defense spending to fund new and bigger social-spending programs, while our military preparedness is already at dangerously low levels. Overall, President Clinton's defense cuts and lack of coherent foreign policy threaten to return us to the "hollow military" experienced under Jimmy Carter. The National Security Restoration Act would:

❖ **Restrict U.N. Command of U.S. Troops**

Codifying the Bush administration's position that dealt with the chain of command for peacekeeping exercises.

❖ **Determine Realistic U.S. Military Needs**

Commissioning an accurate, comprehensive review of military needs for national security, force readiness, and modernization. Former Secretary of Defense Les Aspin's "bottom-up review" of future military needs was widely viewed as advocating reasonable objectives, but providing unreasonable funding to achieve these objectives. What is needed is a new, blue-ribbon panel of outside experts to assess what level of funding would be required to meet our readiness, maintenance, and general operational needs.

❖ **Restore the Budget Firewalls for Defense Spending**

Preventing raiding the defense budget for social-spending programs. Any cuts in defense would go to reducing the deficit.

❖ **Renewed Commitment to a National Missile Defense**

Protecting against rogue nuclear states like North Korea by providing adequate funding for an effective national missile defense to be deployed as soon as possible. It also instructs the Clinton administration not to foreclose national or theater missile defenses in its ongoing Anti-Ballistic Missile Treaty negotiations with the Russians.

❖ **Renew Commitment to a Strong NATO**

Urging the administration to proceed with full NATO partnership discussions with Poland, Hungary, the Czech Republic, and other Central European nations that are striving to meet the criteria of democratic elections, including free-market economies and civilian control of the military.

7. Senior-Citizens Reforms
(The Senior-Citizens Equity Act)

Every year more Americans join the ranks of the elderly. Our tax laws, however, impose harsh penalties on our senior citizens, especially those who continue to work beyond age 65. The Social Security Earnings Limit pushes millions of seniors out of the workforce, and last year's tax hike on Social Security benefits hit many middle-income seniors hard. On top of these financial burdens, many seniors worry about being able to take care of their long-term health-care needs. The Senior-Citizens Equity Act would address these concerns of older Americans:

❖ **Increase the Social Security Earning Limit Threshold**

Under current law, senior citizens between the ages of 65 and 69 lose $1 in Social Security benefits for every $3 they earn above $11,160. This "earnings test" amounts to an additional 33 percent marginal tax rate, on top of existing income taxes. In some instances, this can result in an 85 percent marginal tax rate on a senior's earnings, punishing those who choose to remain productive beyond age of 64.

The seventh bill in our Contract, the Senior-Citizens Equity Act, raises the earning limit threshold to approximately $30,000 over a five-year period. It eliminates the bias against working seniors, allowing them to continue to contribute to our nation's economy.

❖ **Repeal Clinton's Social Security Benefits Tax**

The 1993 Clinton tax law requires senior citizens who earn more than $34,000 (singles) or $44,000 (couples) to pay income taxes on 85 percent of their Social Security benefits. This bill would provide tax relief to middle-class senior citizens by repealing Clinton's tax increases on Social Security benefits. It would lower the amount of Social Security benefits subject to income taxes to 50 percent—the level that existed prior to the 1993 Clinton tax law.

❖ Tax Incentives for Private Long-Term-Care Insurance

This proposal encourages individuals to buy private long-term-care insurance coverage. It allows tax-free withdrawals from IRAs and other pension plans to buy long-term-care insurance and provides a tax deduction to offset the cost of purchasing long-term-care insurance. It also allows accelerated death benefits to be paid from life insurance policies for terminally ill patients or those permanently confined to a nursing home. The proposal helps senior citizens pay for the cost of care in the last years and eliminates financial burdens for them and their families. The Republicans pledge to bring to the floor a plan that treats long-term-care insurance as a tax-free fringe benefit and the same as accident and health insurance. It provides incentives for employers to offer long-term-care insurance plans to their employees.

❖ Senior-Citizen Retirement Communities

This proposal allows housing communities to meet the Fair Housing Amendment Act's "adults-only" housing test if those communities can prove that at least 80 percent of their units are senior occupied. Current law is vague on what constitutes senior housing, and, consequently, lawsuits have been brought against real-estate agents and retirement-community board members.

8. Economic Opportunity/Regulatory Reform
(The Job Creation and Wage Enhancement Act)

Republicans favor lower taxes on the investment that creates jobs and the income people derive from jobs. In order to support more government programs and their bureaucracies, the Democrats have consistently advocated high taxes on both income and capital. Republicans also favor cost-effective regulations to address real risks. Democrats have worked hard to prevent analysis of government regulations to determine their real contribution to our common welfare. For example, the Clean Air Act expressly forbids agencies from weighing economic effects in writing their implementing regulations.

The burden of taxes and regulations on investment created an economic "growth gap" between the historic post-World War II rate of 4 percent real growth per year to a projection of only 2.5 percent real growth through the end of this century. Government-imposed taxes in the form of mandates and regulations have lowered growth and investment in productivity-enhancing capital, which has suppressed wage growth. Cutting taxes on investment and savings will spur greater job creation, and slashing federal red tape will increase worker wages.

Excessive government regulation threatens the competitiveness of American business, stifles entrepreneurial activity, and suppresses economic growth and job creation. Regulations can also have a direct impact on the lives of all Americans—raising the prices they pay for goods and services, restricting the use of their private property, and limiting the availability of credit, among others. The Republican goal with the Job Creation and Wage Enhancement Act is to enhance private-property rights and economic liberty, decentralize and reduce the power

of the state, and make government bureaucrats accountable for the burdens they impose on American workers.

❖ **Capital Gains Tax Cut**

The double taxation of investment income
(dividends are first taxed as profits to a company
and again when distributed as capital gains to the
investor) discourages savings and encourages
borrowing and consumption. The U.S. tax code
imposes a much more onerous tax on capital gains
than our economic competitors, notably Japan and
Germany. A 50 percent exclusion on capital gains
would effectively halve the capital gains tax rate,
spurring investment and job creation.

The Job Creation and Wage Enhancement Act
would also allow investors to index capital gains to
inflation, eliminating taxation on illusory, inflated
dollars. Democrat Party class-war rhetoric to the
contrary, sound economic analysis indicates that
92 percent of the after-tax benefits of lower taxes
on capital accrues to wage earners, not investors.

❖ **Neutral Cost Recovery**

The Job Creation and Wage Enhancement Act's
neutral cost-recovery provision would reduce
business costs across the board by allowing
businesses to depreciate a full 100 percent of the
purchase-price value of their investments by
making investments more affordable. It would
dramatically increase jobs and economic growth. A
recent analysis by the Institute for Policy
Innovation projected that the proposal would
create 2.7 million jobs, produce an additional $3.5

trillion in economic activity by the year 2000, and annually would increase the U.S. gross domestic product by $1 trillion and economic activity by 1.8 percent.

❖ Small-Business Appreciation

In the economic expansion of the Reagan years, small businesses accounted for about 12 million of the 18 million new jobs added to the economy. The Clinton administration has pounded Main Street with an unrelenting stream of new mandates, taxes, and regulations. The following small-business appreciation provisions of the Job Creation and Wage Enhancement Act would provide much needed relief:

- Raising the expensing level from $17,500 to $25,000, allowing small businesses to deduct the first $25,000 they invest in equipment and inventory, encouraging investment and alleviating the cumbersome paperwork of depreciation schedules.

- Clarifying the home-office deduction, allowing taxpayers to qualify if the home office is used (1) exclusively for business purposes, (2) on a regular basis, (3) to perform tasks that could not easily be performed elsewhere, and (4) as an essential part of the taxpayer's business.

- Increase the estate tax exemption from $600,000 to $750,000, thus restoring the value eroded by inflation and making it easier for small-business owners and family farmers to keep their shops and farms in the family.

❖ **Taxpayer Empowerment to**
Reduce Deficit/Debt Buy-Down

The national debt currently exceeds $3.5 trillion,
and each year Congress adds to the debt, spending
billions more than it takes in. The Taxpayer Debt
Buy-Down provision would empower taxpayers to
designate up to 10 percent of their tax liability to a
public-debt reduction fund. This fund would be
strictly earmarked for national debt reduction.
Under the law, Congress would be required to cut
spending equal to the amount designated by the
taxpayers. If these cuts are not realized, an across-
the-board sequester would be imposed.

In the late 1960s and early 1970s, the degree
and scope of federal regulation exploded. Although
the growth of regulation was tamed during the
Reagan administration, it re-accelerated during the
Bush administration and continues to climb under
President Clinton. The number of federal
regulatory agencies in the United States has grown
steadily from less than 10 before 1900 to 56 today.
The number of pages in the Federal Register serves
as an indicator of the amount of new regulation
issued by these agencies annually. In 1993, the
Federal Register numbered more than 70,000
pages—a 47 percent increase over the 1986 Reagan
administration level.

The costs of regulation are as difficult to
measure as the benefits. These costs, which are
much larger than simply the costs of compliance,
include lost opportunities, declining productivity,
and resource misallocations. Robert Hahn and
John Hird recently calculated that in 1988

regulation imposed a net cost of as much as $153 billion on the U.S. economy in terms of lost productivity and lower growth due to resource misallocation. They determined that the average American in 1988 paid $4,000 in excess of the benefits conferred by the regulations—adding to the heavy tax burden imposed by the government. More important, however, regulation is a hidden tax.

❖ Risk Assessment/Cost-Benefit Analysis and Sound Science

Congress is never forced to ensure that the benefits of regulation, better health, and productivity outweigh the costs, lost jobs, and lower wages. Nor does Congress pursue integrated health and safety goals. Instead, Congress and federal regulators often attack whatever health risk has caught the public's attention, even if its regulatory solution exacerbates other health risks. The Job Creation and Wage Enhancement Act will require federal agencies to use up-to-date scientific evidence to assess risks separately and manage them together. Agencies will have to release cost-benefit analyses so that the American public can evaluate the costs of new regulations.

❖ Regulatory Budget

Today's budget deficit is high on the public-policy agenda because it is easily measured and understood. American families can't spend more than they take in, and Congress should live within those same rules. Congress finds its way around Americans' dislike for taxes and deficits by simply forcing American businesses and workers to carry out federal mandates and regulations. The cost of the regulations is no different than a tax—but it doesn't show up in the federal budget. To remedy this, the Republican House will establish a regulatory budget that forces federal agencies to announce the costs their regulations impose on American taxpayers. A cap will then be imposed on those costs of regulations at a point below their current level, forcing agencies to find more cost-effective ways of reaching their goals and to rethink regulatory policies to identify the ones that truly provide more benefits than costs to American workers.

❖ Unfunded Mandate Reforms

The Congressional Budget Office has estimated that the cumulative cost of new regulations imposed on state and local governments between 1983 and 1990 is between $8.9 and $12.7 billion. Unfunded federal mandates remove the ability of state and local governments to direct their tax dollars toward the communities' established priorities. They also impose one-size-fits-all policies on areas as diverse as New York City and rural Iowa. State and local governments resort to higher taxes to meet the costs of unfunded federal mandates. The Job Creation and Wage Enhancement Act will require all legislation to carry an accurate estimate of the costs to state and local governments, and will void any future law that imposes unfunded mandates. It also will cap the costs of mandates below their current level, which will force Congress to prioritize its policies within a mandate budget.

❖ Strengthen Paperwork Reduction Act and Regulatory Flexibility Act

Compliance with federal regulation consumes tens of thousands of hours of labor each year. Employers hiring lawyers to fill out government paperwork must hire fewer workers to produce goods and services. The Republican House will force the federal government to reduce the paperwork burden by five percent and extend the Paperwork Reduction Act to cover paperwork that the federal government mandates employers to produce for third-party use. The Regulatory Flexibility Act will subject to judicial review, so that small businesses can sue to enforce the law.

❖ Compensation for Private-Property Taking

A private-property owner would be entitled to receive compensation for any reduction in the value of property that is a consequence of a limitation on the use of such property imposed by the federal government.

❖ Regulatory Impact Analyses

Requires agencies drafting a major new rule to complete a regulatory impact analysis—an assessment of the potential impact of a regulation based on 23 criteria (e.g., necessity of rule, problem, and how rule will address it, an evaluation of the costs versus benefits).

9. Commonsense Legal Reforms
(The Commonsense Legal Reforms Act)

Our legal system has become burdened with excessive costs and long delays, and no longer serves to expedite justice or ensure fair results. Instead, overuse and abuse of the legal system impose tremendous costs on American society. It has been estimated that each year the United States spends an estimated $300 billion as an indirect cost of the civil justice system. These billions of dollars result from dramatic expansions in the number of cases filed—a tripling of cases in the federal courts alone in the last 30 years. In fact, in 1989 alone, 18 million civil lawsuits were filed in state and federal courts—amounting to one lawsuit for every ten adults. The Commonsense Legal Reforms Act provides the following concrete steps to restore the efficiency and fairness of our civil justice system.

❖ **Discouraging Wasteful Litigation**

One of the most effective ways to ensure that nuisance or frivolous lawsuits are not filed (or that a frivolous defense is not offered) is to require that the loser of a lawsuit pay the winner for the legal fees incurred. The "loser pays" approach encourages careful consideration of the merits of one's case and the exploration of a settlement prior to filing a suit. This fee-shifting provision would be limited to federal diversity cases to ensure that litigants seeking to enforce federal civil rights are not adversely affected. Along the same lines, many lawsuits could be avoided if the parties would just sit down and discuss their differences before going to court. To achieve this first commonsense step, the bill requires claimants to notify the other party prior to filing suit, thus encouraging settlements before resorting to litigation.

❖ Honesty in Evidence

The last decade has witnessed an explosion of abusive practices using rent-an-expert witnesses and unsupported scientific theories. The bill prevents the use of "junk science" by requiring expert testimony to be based on sound scientific theories and bars contingency fees for expert witnesses.

❖ Reasonable Limits on Punitive Damages

It is news to no one that juries have been winging out of control over the past decade in awarding punitive damages far in excess of what is recovered to make a plaintiff whole. Part of the blame rests with the system, because it gives juries very little guidance with which to make such awards. The Commonsense Bill provides these standards by requiring that awards be based on "clear and convincing" evidence of malicious conduct and be limited to three times compensatory damages.

❖ Truth in Attorneys' Fees

Attorneys often operate under a billing arrangement, called a contingency fee, that is based on a percentage of the damages recovered. While this fee arrangement helps some worthy claimants have access to courts, it also creates a situation ripe for abuse by attorneys. To prevent abuse, one way to secure the benefits of contingency fees while protecting unsuspecting plaintiffs is to require attorneys to disclose up front the exact terms of the billing arrangement, document the actual time spent on the case, and allow a client who believes he has been misled to petition the court for redress.

❖ **Legislative Checklist**

The vague and incomplete laws Congress passes today encourage litigation to determine exactly what Congress meant when it spoke on a particular bill. This provision mandates that Congress follow a simple checklist to ensure that new legislation makes clear exactly what is intended, such as whether the new law includes a private right of action, a statute of limitation, or is to be applied retroactively.

❖ **Proportionate Liability**

Under today's liability standards, litigants can go after the "deep pocket" defendants for the full amount of damages—including pain and suffering and punitive damages—even though this party was responsible for only a small fraction of the harm. This standard encourages abusive practices to shake down the deep pockets despite their limited liability. The bill requires apportioning liability on the basis of a defendant's responsibility.

10. Term Limits (The Citizen Legislature Act)

Term limits would eliminate the inevitable consequences of careerism in Congress: a system closed to outsiders wanting to participate and unresponsive to the needs of its constituents. Careerism in Congress is well documented.

The term-limits movement is sweeping the states, winning by overwhelming margins whenever and wherever it is on the ballot. House Republicans respect the rights of the states and respect the rights of citizens to limit the terms of their elected officials. In contrast, then Democrat Speaker of the House Tom Foley filed suit against the voters of Washington State to stop the term-limits initiative they passed almost two years ago. The

House Republicans believe that an issue the magnitude of term limits deserves a national debate.

- Over the past decade, the rate of reelection for House incumbents is 90 percent. In 1992, the so-called year of change, the reelection rate for incumbents was 93 percent. Such numbers do not represent a citizen legislature as envisioned by the Founding Fathers, but rather a body of government with almost identical turnover to that of Britain's House of Lords, whose members are appointed for life.

- An entrenched body of politicians erodes accountability and responsiveness of Congress. An enormous national debt, deficit spending, and political scandals are but a few of the results.

- Although enacting term limits would not be a panacea, it will be the first step to putting our legislative system back on track.

- Term limits have won in every state where they have been placed on the ballot—with average victory margins of 2 to 1. Poll after poll reveals strong support for term limits among the American people; a *Wall Street Journal*/NBC News poll found that 80 percent of Americans favor term limits.

- The Citizen Legislature Act includes a vote on two different term-limit amendments in the first 100 days of a Republican-controlled House. The first would limit the terms of representatives to six years and senators to twelve. The second would impose limits of twelve years in both the House and Senate. Enactment of either would replace career politicians with citizen legislators.

✦ ✦ ✦

THE CONTRACT: GRENADES . . . AND ALTERNATIVES

When first unveiled, elements of the Republican Contract were so controversial that Democrats thought they had been issued a reprieve from impending disaster.

> Thank you, God, for Newt Gingrich. That's the prayer Washington Democrats whisper each night before ducking beneath their covers. Were it not for the pugnacious minority whip, the self-pitying Democrats, facing an electoral stomping, would be without hope and without a clue. Throughout the summer, White House honchos, Democratic National Committee jefes, and Congressional leadership heavies stared dazedly at memos and charts predicting their loses: 30, 40, 50, 60 seats in the House. . . .
>
> Then along came Gingrich. He brought scores of Republican candidates to the steps of the Capitol and had each initial his "Contract With America," a warmed-over stew of Reaganesque policy proposals—tax cuts, more military spending, the anti-choice gag rule. Aha! exclaimed the dejected Democrats. We have a target: Republicans who want to take us back to the 1980s—a time celebrated only in the seminar rooms of the Heritage Foundation. . . .
>
> "Gingrich didn't need to do anything," says one senior DNC official. "If he had kept his mouth shut, the Republicans would have taken over both houses of Congress, no problem. The Contract was such a gift."
>
> —*The Nation*, November 7, 1994

Economists and other experts threw grenades at the Contract: It would explode the deficit. It would rerun the worst excesses of the 1980s. It would favor the rich. Here's a sampling:

> If all the hype about the House Republicans' so-called Contract with America elicits a pervasive sense of deja vu, there's a good reason. We've been here before—exactly 15 years ago. It was a naive, foolhardy fantasy then, and—having spent hundreds of billions of dollars to repair the damage—it's doubly so today. . . .
>
> Now here we go again, with what critics correctly label "Voodoo Two": a promised amendment to balance the budget (conveniently put off for eight years), tax cuts that mainly benefit the wealthy, and pledges to boost a still-bloated defense budget—all to be accomplished within 100 days.
>
> —*San Francisco Chronicle*, November 16, 1994

> The problem is that the Contract calls for tax cuts and tax credits at the same time that it calls for a Constitutional amendment to require a balanced budget. Steering behind an already vigorous business expansion, the Contract would hit the economic accelerator at the same time that it jams on the fiscal brakes. . . .
>
> What most outrages some moderate Republicans is the Contract's projected price tag. The

Republican staff at the House Budget Committee estimates the cost at $190 billion over five years. . . . Although such numbers—$30–40 billion a year—may seem puny against a $1.6 trillion budget, they represent roughly 15 percent of nondefense discretionary spending in 1995.

—*National Journal*, October 22, 1994

It is a vision that looks backward, Reaganism in a rear-view mirror. What this self-styled "Contract with America" says to voters is that these Republicans do not speak candidly. . . .

The Contract is not only reckless but deceptive. The tax cuts on capital gains income, corporate investment, and retirement savings are structured to cost little money during the five-year period for which the Republicans do their accounting. But the proposals are certain to pry open gigantic holes in the budget beyond five years. . . .

Mr. Gingrich promised a positive vision. What voters got instead was duplicitous propaganda.

—*New York Times*, September 28, 1994

An Alternative Contract

In a more serious effort to respond comprehensively to the Republican Contract, the centrist Democratic Leadership Council offered its own 10-point plan in early December 1994 and urged President Clinton to embrace it. Its elements, as outlined by both the Council and *Washington Post* columnist Hobart Rowen, are as follows.

1. A GI Bill for American Workers

This proposal would replace billions of dollars of wasteful or unused worker-training programs with vouchers so that the unemployed could choose their own retraining for a new career.

2. Cut and Invest

Cuts in spending programs and subsidies would be made and reinvested in tax relief and deficit reduction. The emphasis here is to predicate any tax cuts on spending cuts first, an important distinction from the Republican Contract.

3. An Invitation to Trade

A strong emphasis should be placed on creating jobs through regional and global trade expansion, following the passage of both the North American Free Trade Agreement (NAFTA) and the General Agreement on Tariffs and Trade (GATT).

4. Cutting Washington Down to Size

Responsibilities and programs should be shifted from the federal government to states and localities.

5. Health-Care Reform—Take Two

Health-care reform should be pushed again, but on a much more modest and less government-reliant scale than that which was advocated last year by President Clinton and the First Lady.

6. Putting Work First

Welfare would be replaced with a program which ensures that work always pays more than public assistance. Finding jobs for welfare recipients would take precedence over allowing them to spend seemingly endless years in expensive education and job-training programs.

7. Up from Public Housing

Housing programs should emphasize home ownership at low costs rather than rent subsidies.

8. Rolling Back Teen Pregnancy

A moral crusade should be launched in government and throughout society strongly condemning the notion of teens becoming pregnant.

9. Ending the Nuclear Century

The president should work for the reduction of nuclear stockpiles and tough verification to keep these weapons out of the hands of any additional countries.

10. Strengthening America's Hand

The president should reassess America's defense needs and reassure the public that he is committed to an American military that is ready, well-equipped, and second to none.

Columnist Rowen sums up this alternative contract as follows: "The clear focus of these 10 points is to help the average family and the family worker, and not to engage, as would the GOP 'Contract,' in a hemorrhage of tax cutting."

Yet both the criticism and the alternative proposals seem to be bouncing easily off House Speaker Newt Gingrich's armor of self-confidence. In his acceptance speech to fellow Republicans upon his election as Speaker-to-Be, he gleefully rattled off the levels of support for various

Republican Contract proposals as revealed in the following *USA Today* poll of American voters:

tough-crime proposals	88%
balanced-budget amendment	85%
tax cuts	83%
welfare reform	79%
line-item veto	77%
term limits	73%
capital-gains tax cut	58%
tort reform	58%

CHAPTER THREE

THE REPUBLICAN HOUSE OF REPRESENTATIVES

Pictures and Profiles of the New Leaders

SPEAKER OF THE HOUSE
Newt Gingrich

Office: (202) 225-4501; fax: (202) 225-4656

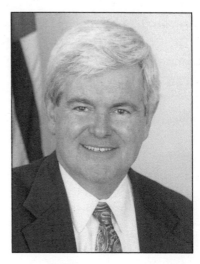

Sixth-District Representative and House Speaker Newt Gingrich of Marietta, Georgia, is currently serving his ninth term in the House of Representatives. His district includes parts of Cobb, Cherokee, North Fulton, DeKalb, and Gwinnett counties. From 1989 to 1994 Gingrich served as Republican whip under long-time minority leader Robert Michel. Michel's decision to retire at the conclusion of the 103d Congress opened the door for Gingrich to assume the leadership position within the House Republicans. Now, having become the first Republican speaker in 40 years, Gingrich has emerged as arguably the second most powerful man in America. It has been a long road.

Gingrich, the son of a career soldier, has never shied away from aggressive opposition to the House Democratic power structure. Political aggressiveness aside, however, the new Speaker is not so easy to categorize. He has been called a "revolutionary centrist" by *Newsweek* and a "thoughtful analyst . . . who gushes with ideas" by the *New York Times*. The *Wall Street Journal*'s Al Hunt described him as "the most pivotal Republican in the land today." Columnist and television commentator Robert Novak said, "More than any other politician, he has had the courage to challenge the political system in Washington."

Gingrich co-founded the Congressional Military Reform Caucus, the Committee Opportunity Society, and the Congressional Space Caucus; he has also served as co-chairman of the House Republican Task Force on Health since the 102d Congress. From 1986 to 1994, he chaired GOPAC, one of the four major national Republican committees.

Gingrich lives in Marietta with his wife, Marianne, with whom he co-authored (with David Drake) the book *Window of Opportunity*. He has two married daughters, Kathy and Jackie.

Gingrich received his bachelor's degree from Emory University and a master's and doctorate in modern European history from Tulane University. He has studied under quality guru Dr. W. Edwards Deming and is an honorary member of the advisory board at the Center for Quality Excellence at the Southern Institute of Technology in Marietta.

Before being elected to Congress in 1978, he taught history and environmental studies at West Georgia College for eight years. In September 1993 Gingrich returned to the classroom as a part-time instructor for a course entitled "Renewing American Civilization" at Kennesaw State College. In January 1994 he moved the course to Reinhardt College (Waleska, Georgia), where he will teach each winter quarter through 1996.

Since his ascension to the House Speakership, Gingrich has become the most analyzed and scrutinized man in America. (One article in a major daily newspaper was called "Inside Newt's Brain.") A representative sample:

> Gingrich knows that he needs to curb his tendency to lob verbal grenades and turn his angry

rhetoric about dismantling the corrupt liberal welfare state into responsible policy. But he has a hard time restraining himself.

—Eleanor Clift, *Newsweek*, November 21, 1994

Don't moderate anything! That's the first trap of inside the beltway: we've got to moderate our tone now that we're here? He [Gingrich] has got to keep firing with both barrels.

—Rush Limbaugh, as quoted in the *New York Times*, December 14, 1994

Gingrich is not a man to waffle. If the logical extension of his draconian brand of welfare reform is to bring back Victorian orphanages, he'll say so. . . . Equivocation in pursuit of bipartisanship is no virtue when the opposition is moving at full partisan speed ahead. It's basic Newtonian physics that Newt can only be countered by a Newt of our own.

—Frank Rich, syndicated columnist, November 18, 1994

[Gingrich's] capitalizing on the media goes far beyond hogging the camera; in fact, the camera seems riveted to him, in part because his oration skills make him a compelling public speaker. He is absolutist, aggressive, hyperbolic, informed, topical, unpredictable, and studied in his use of supercharged symbolic language.

—Katherine Q. Seelye, *New York Times*, December 14, 1994

A few unhappy Republicans and a lot of dumb-founded Democrats may be about to make the mistake with Newt Gingrich that they made with Ronald Reagan way back when to Reagan's abiding good fortune. As they did with Reagan, whose views they detested, they are inclined to misread Gingrich in a way that will lead them to underestimate his political skill. . . . If opponents in both parties insist on fighting their worst fantasy of the man, not the actual Gingrich who is trouble enough, they will be doing him a gigantic favor. They will also lose.

—Meg Greenfield, *Washington Post*,
December 12, 1994

The Gingrich Reading List

In his speech to fellow Republicans following his election as Speaker of the House, Gingrich reverted to his old habits as a college history professor and suggested that all members and their staffs read the following works:

The Declaration of Independence

The Federalist Papers

Democracy in America, by Alexis de Tocqueville

Washington: The Indispensable Man, by James Thomas Flexner (Little Brown, 1969)

Creating a New Civilization: The Politics of the Third Wave, by Alvin and Heidi Toffler (The Progress & Freedom Foundation, 1994)

The Effective Executive, by Peter F. Drucker (Harper & Row, 1966)

Leadership and the Computer, by Mary E. Boone (Prima, 1993)

Working Without a Net: How to Survive and Thrive in Today's High-Risk Business World, by Morris R. Shechtman (Prentice Hall, 1994)

MAJORITY LEADER
Richard K. Armey

Office: (202) 225-7772; fax: (202) 225-7614

Twenty-Sixth District Representative Dick Armey of Copper Canyon, Texas, is serving his sixth term in the House. His district, in the northern suburbs of the Dallas–Fort Worth metroplex, includes Carrolton, Farmers Branch, Richardson, Coppell, Collin County, and most of Denton County.

Armey, who came to the House as a former professor of economics, first gained prominence for his integral role in the formation of a nonpartisan base-closing commission. The commission, when first proposed, was unpopular with both the Pentagon and the Congress, neither of which was eager to relinquish its power over the placement and status of military bases. Armey, however, tirelessly lobbied Congressional and military leaders, working with the joint chiefs of staff and the Armed Services chairman to make the commission a reality. His nonpartisan model has been used since in the more recent round of base closings.

While it is not contained in the Republican Contract with America, another Armey proposal is a flat tax of 17 percent, less certain allowances. In fact, he has gained a national following for his relentless pursuit of this proposal. The Armey plan would devise a federal tax return form the size of a postcard; allow a substantial personal allowance for individuals and dependents; tax remaining income at 17 percent for all Americans; and end all other loopholes as well as withholding. He can be expected to pursue this idea with even greater fervor as majority leader.

Armey earned his bachelor of arts from Jamestown University, his master's from the University of North Dakota, and his doctorate from the University of Oklahoma. He and his wife, Susan, have five children.

Shortly after the election, Armey was asked how Congress would change with Republicans in charge. He replied,

> We believe that there's a great many ways, just a variety of ways all across the Congress, certainly starting with the committee structure and the committee staff, where we can cut down on the number of functionaries, the number of offices and positions, the number of committees, and the number of staff and make this a much leaner, much more efficient, more cost-effective and efficient institution for the public's business. We're beginning to discover, as it were, the amount of, of what should I say, fat that can be trimmed off as to strengthen the muscle of this congressional enterprise.

MAJORITY WHIP
Thomas DeLay

Office: (202) 225-5951; fax: (202) 225-5241

Twenty-Second District Representative Tom DeLay of Sugar Land, Texas, is serving his sixth term in the House. His district spans from southwest Houston to parts of Fort Bend and Brazoria Counties and to the Clear Lake area of southeast Houston.

DeLay, member of the Congressional Space Caucus, is widely recognized as a conservative firmly committed to reductions in government budgets and programs. His accomplishments at the local and national levels have gained him recognition as a legislator who can work with both sides of the aisle to obtain positive results.

DeLay's conservative voting record has earned him the Taxpayers' Friend Award from the National Taxpayers Union and 100 percent ratings from *New American* and *Christian Voice* magazines. He has received a Golden Bulldog Award from the Watchdog of the Treasury for his efforts to cut federal spending and reduce the deficit, and a National Security Leadership Award from the Coalition of Peace Through Strength for his commitment to national defense. He has also consistently received high marks from the U.S. Chamber of Commerce for his pro-business stance.

DeLay made his start in politics in 1978, when he became the first Republican to represent Fort Bend County in the Texas House of Representatives, where he served for six years.

Born in Loredo, Texas, on April 8, 1947, DeLay spent much of his childhood in Venezuela, where his father was an oil-drilling contractor. He returned to Texas for high school, attended Baylor University, and in 1970 graduated from the University of Houston. DeLay and his wife, Christine, have one daughter, Danielle, who attends college in Texas. He is a member of the Sugar Creek Baptist Church.

COMMITTEES

AGRICULTURE
Chairman, Pat Roberts

Office: (202) 225-2715; fax: (202) 225-5375

First District Representative Pat Roberts of Dodge
City, Kansas, is currently
serving his eighth term.
His district covers 66 counties and the western two-
thirds of Kansas.

As a leader of govern-
mental reform, Roberts or-
ganized the bipartisan
Congressional Caucus on
Unfunded Mandates to
eliminate the practice of
forcing state and local gov-
ernments to shoulder the cost of federal mandates.

As a leader of Congressional reform, Roberts' efforts
have curbed members' bounced checks at the House
bank, unpaid restaurant bills, patronage in the House post
office, perks, and free mail. He has been recognized by the
National Taxpayers Union and other nonpartisan watchdog groups for his votes against higher taxes and deficit
spending. Roberts has also been a leader in the fight to
eliminate nonessential spending in Congress, including
grants to special-interest caucuses. He is a strong voice for
agriculture and is the author of numerous provisions of
major farm legislation to assist producers. Roberts has
also focused much of his career on halting the erosion of

essential government services in transportation, finance, health care, and education.

Roberts is a fourth-generation Kansan, born April 20, 1936, in Topeka. He is the son of the late Wes Roberts, chairman of the Republican National Committee under President Eisenhower. His great-grandfather, J. W. Roberts, founded the *Oskaloosa Independent*, the state's second oldest newspaper. Following his graduation from Kansas State University in 1958, Roberts served four years with the U.S. Marine Corps and was the editor of a weekly newspaper. Roberts and his wife, Franki, have three children, David, Ashleigh, and Anne-Wesley.

The *Wichita Eagle* had this to say about Representative Roberts: "He takes no prisoners when riled by anything he perceives to be anti-agriculture. Armed with a quick wit and an encyclopedic knowledge on the topic, he can win most debates."

The *Hutchinson News* writes, "Roberts is well known in Washington for agricultural acumen and hard-nosed conservatism."

APPROPRIATIONS
Chairman, Bob Livingston

Office: (202) 225-3015; fax: (202) 225-0739

First District Representative Bob Livingston of New Orleans, Louisiana, is currently serving his tenth term. His district includes most of the suburbs of New Orleans as well as portions of Jefferson Parish, St. Tammany Parish, and the Florida Parishes.

Livingston cites as his chief priority the control of federal spending. His efforts have earned him awards from both the Watchdog of the Treasury and the National Association of Businessmen. Livingston is a strong supporter of the line-item veto, which is part of the House Republicans' Contract with America.

Representative Livingston's years as a prosecutor in the U.S. Attorney's office have helped to shape his political agenda. He has spent much of his career working to improve the criminal-justice system and increase penalties for career criminals. He supports the so-called "Three Strikes and You're Out" legislation as well as the death penalty.

Livingston, an advocate of a strong national defense, believes that the Clinton administration has cut defense spending too far and too fast. He has worked to stop the cuts to America's military, especially in the wake of the Persian Gulf War and recent incidents in Korea, Somalia, and Bosnia.

Livingston was born in Colorado Springs, Colorado, and moved to Louisiana at an early age. He earned both his bachelor of arts and his law degree from Tulane University and is a graduate of the Loyola University Institute of Politics. He served the U.S. Navy as an enlisted man from 1961 to 1967. Livingston and his wife, Suzie, have four children, Shep, Richard, David, and Suzie.

BANKING AND FINANCIAL SERVICES
(FORMERLY BANKING, FINANCE, AND URBAN AFFAIRS)
Chairman, Jim Leach

Office: (202) 225-6576; fax: (202) 225-1278

First District Representative Jim Leach of Davenport, Iowa, is currently serving his tenth term. His district covers eight counties in eastern Iowa, including Davenport and Cedar Rapids.

Leach is known as a moderate Republican but one who votes conservatively on fiscal issues. As a member of the Banking Committee, much of his legislative work has been in this arena.

Leach's market-oriented economic philosophy stems from his experience running his family's propane business, during which time he learned first-hand the detrimental effects of governmental regulation on business. He has been a leader on regulatory-reform issues. His "maverick" reputation and independent streak is likely to make for interesting times at the newly named Banking and Financial Services Committee. If the past is any guide, neither party can expect an automatic endorsement or condemnation of its proposals by Leach.

Representative Leach earned his bachelor of arts in political science from Princeton University and his master's in Soviet politics from Johns Hopkins. He and his wife, Elisabeth, have two children, Gallagher and Jenny.

BUDGET
Chairman, John R. Kasich

Office: (202) 225-5355

Twelfth District Representative John Kasich of Westerville, Ohio, is currently serving his seventh term. His district covers the eastern portion of Columbus and stretches north to Delaware county and east to the city of Newark.

Kasich has placed tremendous effort into the fight to shrink the size and cost of government. As the ranking Republican on the Budget Committee in the last Congress, Kasich led the efforts to develop alternatives to the Clinton budgets for fiscal years 1994 and 1995. His "cutting spending first" budget for fiscal year 1994 proposed $430 billion in deficit reduction without a tax increase. His proposed 1995 alternative budget would not only produce lower deficits than the president's, but also deliver the middle-class tax cut that Clinton has promised but never delivered.

Kasich's budgetary work has been met with praise from a diverse field of media pundits. Nationally syndicated columnist David Broder commended the cutting-spending-first proposal as both specific and serious. Similar accolades have come from the *New York Times*, *Washington Post*, and many other periodicals.

During his seven terms in the House, Kasich has acquired expertise in foreign affairs. He was appointed by President Reagan to monitor the elections in El Salvador and has met with leaders around the world in an effort to increase understanding and cooperation.

The *Cincinnati Post* describes Kasich's role in the new Congress this way: "The 42-year-old Kasich and fellow House members Dick Armey, Tom DeLay, and Bob Walker are at the core of Gingrich's inner circle."

USA Today predicts that "while incoming House Speaker Newt Gingrich and others chart a course for the first Republican-controlled House in four decades, the key to their success may well rest with Representative John Kasich of Ohio."

Writing in *U.S. News and World Report,* Gloria Borger sized up Kasich as "a logical descendant of Reagan-era conservatism: he calls himself a supply-side deficit hawk. The contradiction in terms handily synthesizes both wings of the party—and allows Kasich to bridge the divide between moderate and conservative Republicans."

Kasich earned his degree in political science from Ohio State University.

COMMERCE
(FORMERLY ENERGY AND COMMERCE)
Chairman, Thomas J. Bliley Jr.

Office: (202) 225-2815; fax: (202) 225-0011

Seventh District Representative Thomas J. Bliley Jr. of Richmond, Virginia, is currently serving his eighth term. His district includes northern Chesterfield County; the western part of Richmond; northeast and western Henrico County; western Spotsylvania County; all of Orange, Madison, and Culpepper counties; and northern Albemarle County.

While in Congress, Bliley has worked to limit government's impact on business. He fought against the Clinton health-care plan, especially the employer mandates and sanctions. His efforts on behalf of the business community have not gone unnoticed. He has been named a Guardian of Small Business by the National Federation of Small Businesses and has received praise from numerous other organizations, including the National Association of Retail Druggists, the Richmond Bar Association, the Virginia Cable Television Association, and the American Security Council.

Bliley has also been a leader in the attempt to limit wasteful federal spending. His commitment to balancing the federal budget has earned him a Golden Bulldog Award, which is awarded yearly by the National Watchdog of the Treasury.

Bliley earned his bachelor of arts in history from Georgetown University. He served three years in the U.S. Navy, where he earned the rank of lieutenant.

Bliley and his wife, Mary Virginia, have two children, Jerry and Mary Vaughan, and two grandchildren.

ECONOMIC AND EDUCATIONAL OPPORTUNITIES (FORMERLY EDUCATION AND LABOR)
Chairman, William F. Goodling

Office: (202) 225-5836; fax: (202) 225-1000

Nineteenth District Representative Bill Goodling of Jacobus, Pennsylvania, is currently serving his eleventh term. His district stretches from the Mason-Dixon Line north and includes the cities of York, Harrisburg, and Carlisle.

Goodling, who prior to public service was an educator and administrator in the Pennsylvania public school system, has spent much of his Congressional career working to improve the educational system. He was instrumental in securing early enactment of the National Literacy Act, which was directed at cost-effectively combating illiteracy through the coordination of national, state, and local efforts. One of Goodling's programs expanded under this act was an intergenerational literacy program called Even-Start.

During the 103d Congress, Goodling managed to institute tough new standards for Head Start and strengthen its parental-involvement component. He worked for improved coordination of services, flexibility, quality standards, and parental involvement in Goals 2000 and the Elementary and Secondary Education Act.

Goodling has also sought through legislative initiative to improve the jobs climate in the United States by reducing the regulatory burden on business and expanding tax incentives.

Goodling earned his bachelor of science from the University of Maryland and his master's in education from Western Maryland College. He served in the U.S. Army from 1945 to 1948, based in Japan. He and his wife, Hilda, have two children, Todd and Jennifer.

Goodling recently outlined his goals as chair of the Economic and Educational Opportunities Committee as follows:

> My goals for the committee emphasize two overarching themes that are central to the Republican Contract with America.
>
> First, we must empower Americans through local decisions. People, not the federal government, should make the key decisions affecting their lives. This means driving decisions closer to the customer, . . . letting employers and employees make decisions about what is best for them, not decisions made by government mandates and regulations. In terms of education policy, it means local control and putting confidence in parents, teachers, administrators, school boards, and local officials to make the best decisions about how their children will be educated.
>
> Second, we must provide quality solutions. I fundamentally question whether what the federal government provides, across the board, is quality. In a practical sense, this means a comprehensive process of reviewing current

government programs, laws, and regulations. If they aren't working, either reform them, replace them, or throw them out entirely.

If my chairmanship is truly going to be about local decisions and quality solutions, old habits will have to be dramatically changed.

GOVERNMENT REFORM AND OVERSIGHT (FORMERLY GOVERNMENT OPERATIONS)
Chairman, William F. (Bill) Clinger Jr.

Office: (202) 225-5121; fax: (202) 225-4681

First elected in 1978, Fifth District Representative Bill Clinger of Warren, Pennsylvania, is currently serving his ninth term. His district is in the north-central part of Pennsylvania and includes the Nittany Valley, Oil City, and Lewisburg.

Clinger has earned a reputation as a leading proponent of more open government and higher ethical standards. One of his most provocative ideas for restoring the public's confidence in its elected officials is to install a clock in the Congress that will keep track of the national debt. He believes that this constant reminder of how government is "passing the buck" may help slow the free-spending habits of his colleagues.

Clinger earned his bachelor of arts from Johns Hopkins and his law degree from the University of Virginia. He served as an intelligence officer in the U.S. Navy from 1951 to 1955. He and his wife, Julia, have four children, Eleanor, William F. III, James, and Julia.

HOUSE OVERSIGHT
(FORMERLY HOUSE ADMINISTRATION)
Chairman, William (Bill) Thomas

Office: (202) 225-2915; fax: (202) 225-8798

Twenty-First District Representative Bill Thomas of Bakersfield, California, is currently serving his ninth term. His district covers the southern part of the Central Valley of California and includes Bakersfield, Tulare, Porterville, and Visalia, as well as Edwards Air Force Base.

Thomas's career in Congress can be described as a crusade to improve the ethics and integrity of the House and ensure that members live by the same laws that they impose on everyone else. He pushed for the investigations of both the House post office and bank. He has been instrumental in passing legislation to reform the House, including a bill to stop the practice of representatives sending taxpayer-financed mass mailings to addresses outside their districts. He has also worked on campaign-finance reform.

Thomas earned his bachelor's and his master's from San Francisco State University. He and his wife, Sharon, have two children, Chris and Amelia.

Politics in America 1994 describes Thomas as a man who "relishes the role of partisan strategist. He is one of the best in the house at watching a floor debate or a committee meeting and taking in all the political implications. He has long employed his combative style to advantage, not just on the floor but also in the Ways and Means Committee—where Republicans have often preferred to avoid public confrontations."

INTERNATIONAL RELATIONS (FORMERLY FOREIGN AFFAIRS)
Chairman, Benjamin A. Gilman

Office: (202) 225-3776; fax: (202) 225-2541

First elected in 1972, Twentieth District Representative Benjamin A. Gilman of Middletown, New York, is currently serving his eleventh term in the House of Representatives. His district encompasses all or part of the counties of Rockland, Orange, Westchester, and Sullivan.

Gilman won acclaim in 1978 for his successful efforts to bring about prisoner exchanges with East Germany, Mozambique, Cuba, and several other nations. "Ben Gilman sees his political life as one long effort to help individuals in distress," noted *People* magazine in a 1978 profile.

In 1980, Gilman successfully fought to have 30 Americans freed from political imprisonment by the Cuban government. The internationally acclaimed journalist Jacobo Timmermann noted in his autobiography that Gilman paid him a humanitarian visit in his prison cell in junta-ruled Argentina. In the days prior to the collapse of the Soviet Union, Gilman was known as perhaps the premier Congressional champion of the Pentecostals, Ukrainians, Poles, Soviet Jews, and other ethnic and religious groups denied their basic freedoms and the right to emigrate.

He is also noted for his efforts in the war on drugs. In the mid-1970s, he co-founded the House Select Committee on Narcotics, on which he was the ranking Republican from 1977 to 1989. Gilman has visited the leading drug-producing nations of the world and has been out front on his hard-line, antidrug stance at conferences from London to Vienna. A profile in the *Rockland Journal News* (April 2, 1989) said that Gilman views the fight against drugs as "dominating the moral, ethical, and political fibers of the country."

Gilman earned his bachelor of science from the University of Pennsylvania and his law degree from New York School of Law. He served in the Army Air Corps from 1942 to 1945. He was a member of the New York State Assembly from 1967 until his election to Congress. Gilman and his wife, Rita, have five children.

JUDICIARY
Chairman, Henry J. Hyde

Office: (202) 225-4561; fax: (202) 225-1240

Sixth District Representative Henry J. Hyde of Bensenville, Illinois, is currently serving his eleventh term in the House of Representatives. His district encompasses much of the area surrounding Chicago, including the suburbs of Park Ridge, Villa Park, Wheaton, Bensenville, Addison, Wood Dale, Des Plaines, Glen Ellyn, Lombard, Elmhurst, Bloomingdale, and Elk Grove Village.

Hyde has become one of the most respected members of the House, where even those who disagree with his staunchly conservative positions on abortion and other issues do not deny his sincerity and integrity. Yet Hyde does on occasion break ranks with conservative orthodoxy; for example, he supported the 1992 Family Leave Act over the objection of President Bush and most fellow Republicans.

As chairman of the House Judiciary Committee, Hyde will play a central role in responding to one of the primary concerns of the 1994 voter: crime. On issues from tort reform to eliminating excessive death penalty appeal, Americans are in for major changes with Henry Hyde controlling the gavel.

Hyde earned his bachelor of science from Georgetown University and his law degree from Loyola. He served in the U.S. Navy from 1944 to 1946 and in the reserves until 1968. He was a member of the Illinois legislature from 1967 until being elected to Congress.

NATIONAL SECURITY (FORMERLY ARMED SERVICES)
Chairman, Floyd D. Spence

Office: (202) 225-2452; fax: (202) 225-2455

Second District Representative Floyd D. Spence of Lexington, South Carolina, is currently serving his thirteenth term. His district covers all of Allendale, Barnwell, Hampton, Jasper, and Lexington counties, as well as parts of Aiken, Beaufort, Calhoun, Colleton, Orangeburg, and Richland counties.

As a leader in the fight to reduce the federal budget, Spence in 1971 became the first House member to sponsor a balanced-budget Constitutional amendment.

As the ranking Republican of the Armed Services Committee, Spence led the fight to limit proposed defense spending cuts, preferring, he says, "responsible downsizing rather than drastic cuts." He vows to continue that fight now as chairman of the National Security Committee.

Spence was born in Columbia, South Carolina, and attended Lexington High School. He attended the University of South Carolina, where he received his bachelor of arts (English) and law degree. He served the U.S. Navy from 1952 until he retired in 1985 as a captain in the Naval Reserve.

Spence and his first wife, the late Lula Handcock Drake Spence, had four sons, David, Zack, Benjamin, and

Caldwell. On July 3, 1988, less than two months after undergoing a double-lung transplant, he married the former Deborah E. Williams of Lexington, South Carolina.

Spelling out his goals as committee chairman, Spence said,

> I will be working to reverse the past two years of neglect of our nation's military. In the short time since our triumph in the Persian Gulf, we have witnessed the slow but steady deterioration of our military capabilities as a result of budget cuts, over-commitment of a shrinking force to peacekeeping and humanitarian missions of questionable national interest, and the dramatically increased use of dwindling defense resources to pay for nondefense programs.
>
> We face some important national-security challenges ahead, and I look forward to working with the newly elected House Republican majority to ensure that the United States military remains fully ready and capable to meet the challenges of an uncertain post–Cold War world.

PUBLIC LANDS AND RESOURCES (FORMERLY NATURAL RESOURCES)
Chairman, Don Young

Office: (202) 225-5456; fax: (202) 225-4370

First elected to the House in 1970, Representative Don Young of Fort Yukon, Alaska, is serving his twelfth term. His district encompasses the entire state of Alaska.

Young is a development-minded conservative who believes that America should rely on its own, rather than on imported, natural resources. He has pressed for exploratory oil drilling in Alaska's National Wildlife Refuge and on the North Slope, fought to continue full logging of the Tongass Forest, and tried to stop the Alaska Lands Act of 1980.

Although suffering setbacks in those legislative battles, Young has nonetheless enjoyed some successes. He worked for passage of legislation, supported by West Coast fishing fleets, that eliminated monofilament driftnet fishing. He also helped block reform of the 1872 Mining Law, which would have made obtaining a mining claim increasingly difficult.

Young earned his bachelor of arts from Chico State University in California. He served in the U.S. Army from 1955 to 1956. He and his wife, Lula, have two children.

RULES
Chairman, Gerald B. Solomon

Office: (202) 225-5614; fax: (202) 225-1168

Twenty-Second District Representative Gerald Solomon
of Glens Falls, New York, is
serving his ninth term in the
House of Representatives.
His district includes much of
the Hudson Valley and most
of Essex County and Lake
Placid, as well as suburban
Albany.

Solomon, a strong parti-
san Republican, has a solidly
conservative voting record.
He is a supporter of the line-
item veto, the balanced budget amendment, and tough
anticrime and antidrug measures.

Solomon has fought to prevent lawbreakers from receiving government subsidies. In the early 1980s he sponsored a bill that cut off college aid for young men who
refused to register for the draft. He also pushed a measure
in 1992 that cut off college aid to first-time narcotics offenders who refuse drug counseling; second-time offenders were cut off for good. In 1990, Solomon sponsored an
amendment that halted highway funding for states that
did not suspend the driver's licenses of convicted drug offenders.

Solomon, currently the Republican's deputy whip, previously served on the House Veterans Affairs Committee
and the Foreign Affairs Committee. He is a member of the
House Task Force on National Defense Policy and mem-

ber and former chairman of the House Task Force on American Prisoners of War and Missing in Southeast Asia. Former President Ronald Reagan appointed him as a Congressional advisor to the U.N. Session on Disarmament. Since 1982, Solomon has served as the Congressional delegate to the North Atlantic Assembly and currently is that organization's chairman of the Political Foreign Affairs Committee.

Solomon earned his bachelor of arts from Saint Lawrence University. He was a U.S. Marine from 1952 to 1954. He and his wife, Freda, have five children.

SCIENCE
(FORMERLY SCIENCE, SPACE, AND TECHNOLOGY)
Chairman, Robert S. Walker

Office: (202) 225-2411; fax: (202) 225-2484

Sixteenth District Representative Robert S. Walker of East Petersburg, Pennsylvania, is currently serving his tenth term in the House. His district includes most of Lancaster County and part of Chester County.

Walker is seen as an innovator in the Congress. One of his ideas, the debt buydown plan, received national attention. The plan, endorsed by George Bush at the 1992 Republican National Convention, would give taxpayers the ability to designate up to 10 percent of their income tax to deficit reduction and require that all spending, save Social Security and debt service, be cut by that percentage. Besides giving taxpayers a direct say over how their tax dollars are spent, Walker contends that, if adopted, his bold plan would reduce the deficit substantially.

As the ranking Republican on the Science, Space, and Technology Committee, Walker consistently supported America's space program, including the space station. He wrote the law to establish the National Space Council and has proposed a Cabinet-level department of science, space, energy, and technology.

Walker said this about his rise to chairman of the Science Committee:

> I am looking forward with great enthusiasm to
> assuming the chairmanship of the House Sci-
> ence Committee. Having served as a member
> of the committee for 18 years, six as the ranking
> Republican, I am eager to pursue an agenda
> that will reflect future-oriented policies. The
> competitiveness of our country in global mar-
> kets will depend on good science and advanced
> technology. Our committee will showcase poli-
> cies that will build our scientific base, enhance
> our technological prowess, extend our reach in
> outer space, and strengthen our economy by
> developing and defining the jobs of the future.

Walker earned his bachelor of arts from Millersville
University and his master's from the University of
Delaware. He is married to the former Sue Albertson.

SMALL BUSINESS
Chairwoman, Jan Meyers

Office: (202) 225-2865; fax: (202) 225-0554

Third District Representative Jan Meyers of Overland Park, Kansas, is serving her sixth term in the House. Her district includes Kansas City and Johnson County plus most of Douglas and Miami counties.

Meyers, who has earned a reputation as a moderate, supports legalized abortion and joined with other moderate Republicans to draft an alternative to President Clinton's health-care initiative. She also supported Clinton's plan to aid Russia.

Meyers is the recipient of numerous awards and honors as a result of her public service and legislative record. She has received seven consecutive Golden Bulldog awards from the Watchdog of the Treasury for her fiscal votes to cut the deficit and eliminate wasteful spending. The National Taxpayers Union has presented her with its Taxpayers' Friend Award for her votes to cut spending and her opposition to tax increases. For her key votes against Congressional pay raises and wasteful government spending, Citizens Against Government Waste has named Meyers a Taxpayer Hero four years running.

The business community has also recognized Meyers for her strong record in support of free enterprise and small business. She was named Guardian of Small Business four consecutive times by the National Federation of Independent Business (NFIB) and received the Spirit of Enterprise Award from the U.S. Chamber of Commerce in 1988, 1989, and 1991.

Myers earned her bachelor of arts from the University of Nebraska. She and her husband, Dutch, have two children, Valerie and Phillip.

TRANSPORTATION AND INFRASTRUCTURE (FORMERLY PUBLIC WORKS AND TRANSPORTATION)
Chairman, Bud Shuster

Office: (202) 225-2431; fax: (202) 225-2486

Ninth District Representative Bud Shuster of Everett, Pennsylvania, is currently serving his seventh term in the House. His district is primarily the towns of the Pennsylvania Appalachian Mountains.

Shuster, with his vociferous opposition to government regulation and taxation, is known as one of the most consistent conservatives in the House. However, much of his legislative success comes from his efforts at improving the nation's deteriorating infrastructure.

Shuster worked with both parties on the Public Works and Transportation Committee to push through transportation and water projects. He is proud of the construction of U.S. Highway 220, which he pushed through Congress; a portion of the highway has even been named after him in recognition of his efforts. He has also been the principal author of numerous pieces of infrastructure legislation, including the Surface Transportation Act of 1982, the Surface Transportation and Uniform Relocation Assistance Act of 1987, and the landmark Intermodal Surface Transportation Efficiency Act of 1991—all which have continued his tradition of creating transportation arteries that facilitate commerce.

Shuster earned his bachelor of science from the University of Pittsburgh, his master's from Duquesne, and his doctorate from American University. He served in the U.S. Army from 1954 to 1956. Shuster and his wife, Patricia, have five children.

VETERANS AFFAIRS
Chairman, Bob Stump

Office: (202) 225-4576; fax: (202) 225-6328

Third District Representative Bob Stump of Tolleson, Arizona, is currently serving his tenth term in the House. His district stretches from the west side of Phoenix to cover most of the northwest portion of the state.

Stump has long been a leader in issues affecting veterans. As the ranking Republican in the last Congress, he worked well with the Democratic chairman of the Veterans Affairs Committee and was able to push through many of his bills and ideas. He has continuously supported full funding of the Pentagon and is critical of the recent steep cuts in defense.

Stump votes a solidly conservative line, against big government and spending, for lower taxes, a balanced budget, and a strong and well-prepared national defense.

Stump earned his bachelor of science from Arizona State University. He served in the U.S. Navy during World War II, from 1943 until 1946. He has three children.

WAYS AND MEANS
Chairman, Bill Archer

Office: (202) 225-2571; fax: (202) 225-4381

Seventh District Represen- tative Bill Archer of Hous- ton, Texas, is currently serving his thirteenth term in the House. His district, which includes portions of the Houston suburbs, has been described as perhaps the most Republican dis- trict in the country.

First elected to Con- gress in 1970, Archer is both an economic and so- cial conservative. He is committed to curtailing federal spending and eliminating the federal budget deficit. Archer favors giving the president the line-item veto, which, he believes, could curtail the unchecked pork barrel spending that continually busts the budget. He has also sponsored proposals for balanced-budget amend- ments every year since he was first elected. Archer hopes to pass a series of bills that would trim nearly $80 billion from the federal budget over the next five years. As chair- man of the House Ways and Means Committee, he be- comes one of the most influential members of Congress, dominating the agenda on all tax legislation, including cuts and reforms. This adds new weight to his suggestion in the past that a national sales tax should be considered in lieu of the federal income tax.

Archer's fiscal conservatism has earned him the Free Congress Foundation's Sound Dollar Award and the Watchdog of the Treasury's Golden Bulldog Award.

Archer received his bachelor's and law degree from the University of Texas. He served in the U.S. Air Force in Korea from 1951 until 1953. He and his wife, Sharon, have seven children.

PERMANENT SELECT COMMITTEE ON INTELLIGENCE
Chairman, Larry Combest

Office: (202) 225-4005; fax: (202) 225-9615

Nineteenth District Representative Larry Combest of Lubbock, Texas, is currently serving his sixth term. His district, which includes the cities of Amarillo, Lubbock, Odessa, and Midland, covers a sprawling 400-mile-wide section of the Texas Panhandle that sweeps through the South Plains and into the Permian Basin.

Combest, who was raised on a farm in West Texas, is the ranking Republican on the Agriculture Committee. He has worked to make government less burdensome on his constituents and on the nation's agricultural community. His efforts have gained him the admiration of many in his community, including the *Amarillo Globe-News*, which wrote: "Combest . . . has gained the reputation of an expert on farm issues." The *Hereford Brand* commented that "if the United States House had more representatives like [Combest], we could solve a lot of this country's problems."

Combest has worked to curb the excessive federal spending. On his first day in Congress, he cosponsored a Constitutional amendment to require a balanced federal budget. He has consistently received a 100 percent rating from the National Federation of Independent Business. He has also received numerous awards from taxpayers and business associations for his efforts to make government less burdensome.

Combest received his bachelor of business administration from West Texas State University in 1969. He and his wife, Sharon, have two grown children.

Shortly after the November 8, 1994, election, the *Washington Post* reported that as chairman of the Permanent Select Committee on Intelligence, Combest

> plans to investigate whether top CIA officials intentionally misled several senior Republican members who between 1988 and 1992 repeatedly asked about loss of U.S.-paid Soviet agents.
>
> It was not until confessed spy Aldrich M. Ames was arrested . . . that Republican committee members learned that at the time they had asked their questions, agency officials already knew that more than a dozen of the CIA's Soviet agents had been killed or arrested and that many more intelligence operations had been exposed.

CHAPTER FOUR

THE REPUBLICAN SENATE

Pictures and Profiles of the New Leaders

MAJORITY LEADER
Robert (Bob) Dole

Office: (202) 224-6521; fax: (202) 224-8952

Bob Dole is currently serving his fifth term as U.S. senator from Kansas. A decorated and wounded combat veteran of World War II, this towering national figure has a distinguished record of public service that spans four decades.

Born and raised on the plains of western Kansas, Dole is a tough, commonsense conservative from America's heartland. Few in Washington can match his experience: Senate majority leader, chairman of the Senate Finance Committee, candidate for president, nominee for vice president, member of the House of Representatives, chairman of the Republican Party, state legislator, and county attorney.

Dole's leadership ability has been recognized by many from both sides of the aisle. According to former President George Bush, Dole "has shown where the leadership really is now in this country in terms of party." Dole's effectiveness as a consensus builder and his commitment to deficit reduction have earned him the admiration of Republicans, Independents, and Democrats alike. Scripps Howard News Service has called Dole "a legislator par excellence—a master of the art of compromise, a bare knuckles negotiator, and a believer in the possible." In fact, former Democratic presidential candidate Paul Tsongas has declared, "If I were Bill Clinton, job number one would be: reach out to Bob Dole and cut a deal on the deficit." According to *Congressional Quarterly*, "it is against his performance and ability to use power that Senate leaders in the foreseeable future will be judged."

During World War II, Dole was a platoon leader in the legendary Tenth Mountain Division in Italy. In 1945, he was gravely wounded on the battlefield and was later twice decorated for heroic achievement. His decorations include two Purple Hearts and a Bronze Star with Oakleaf Cluster.

Dole is married to Elizabeth Hanford Dole, president of the American Red Cross. He also has a daughter, Robin, who resides in Washington, D.C.

MAJORITY WHIP
Trent Lott

Office: (202) 224-6253; fax: (202) 224-2262

Trent Lott is currently serving only his second term as junior senator from Mississippi. His skills as a legislator and politician, as well as his commitment to conservative policies, have enabled him to rise quickly in the Republican leadership.

First elected to the U.S. House of Representatives in 1972, he became the youngest member to have ever served on the Judiciary Committee, where, in 1973, he loyally defended President Nixon during the impeachment proceedings. In 1980 he was elected House Republican whip, a post he held until his election to the Senate in 1988.

Lott's voting record is one of the Senate's most conservative on both cultural and fiscal issues. An adherent of deregulation and supply-side economics, he has a resolute dislike of taxes and big government and has voted to cut both. Lott joined with Senator Phil Gramm to propose $178 billion in spending cuts. He believes in a strong national defense and an assertive foreign policy.

Lott was born in 1941 in Grenada, Mississippi. He attended the University of Mississippi, where he received a bachelor's degree in public administration and a law degree. He and his wife, Patricia, have two children.

COMMITTEES

AGRICULTURE, NUTRITION, AND FORESTRY
Chairman, Richard Lugar

Richard Lugar is currently serving his fourth term as U.S. senator from Indiana.

Lugar is recognized in the Senate as a leader on issues affecting the nation's agricultural sector. He has spearheaded efforts to expand export markets, reform outmoded subsidy programs, and restructure the wasteful federal bureaucracy at the U.S. Department of Agriculture. Senate Majority Leader Bob Dole has said of Lugar: "When Dick speaks, people listen—and they get results."

Lugar was an architect of the landmark 1987 Agricultural Credit Act, which helped forestall a potential crash of the ailing Farm Credit System. The act was modeled after the 1970s loan-guarantee packages for Chrysler Corporation and New York City, which, co-authored by Lugar, ensured that tax dollars loaned were repaid.

Lugar also has a well-earned reputation as a fiscal conservative. He supports the pro-growth policies of low taxes and tight purse strings; he also advocates a balanced budget amendment and a presidential line-item veto. Lugar, known by his colleagues for discipline and fiscal prudence, has maintained a 98 percent voting attendance record and has voluntarily returned more that $2.4 million in unspent office funds.

The National Taxpayers Union has cited fiscally conservative Lugar for "courage and leadership." He voted to curb expanding federal entitlement expenditures, a vote that the *Washington Post* described as "the first major test of support for curtailing programs that have been kept off-limits to Congressional budget-cutters."

As chairman of the Foreign Relations Committee during the 99th Congress (1985–1986), Lugar restored that committee's power and eminence, prompting the *New York Times* to call him the "most influential Republican voice on foreign policy on Capitol Hill."

Lugar successfully led the 1988 Senate ratification of the historic INF treaty with the Soviet Union, which for the first time reduced the number of nuclear weapons. He followed this four years later as manager of the Senate ratification of the START treaty.

Senator Lugar has spoken out against international tyrants. In 1986, he entered the crucible of the Philippine presidential election when he recognized Corazon Aquino as the legitimate winner. By spotlighting the corrupt activities of then-President Ferdinand Marcos and his supporters, Lugar ultimately convinced President Reagan to back Aquino.

As the former mayor of Indianapolis and president of the National League of Cities (1970–1971), Lugar is an expert in economic development, housing, and other urban issues. As the chief executive of his hometown from 1968–1975, he revolutionized the very form and function of Indianapolis by unifying its downtown and urban neighborhoods with surrounding suburban communities.

Lugar was born April 4, 1932, in Indianapolis. He graduated first in his class, both at Shortridge High School and Denison University. He was a Rhodes Scholar and served in the U.S. Navy from 1957 to 1960.

While at Denison, Lugar served as co-president of the student body with his future wife, Charlene Smeltzer. They married September 8, 1956, and have four sons and six grandchildren.

APPROPRIATIONS
Chairman, Mark Hatfield

Office: (202) 224-3753; fax: (202) 224-0276

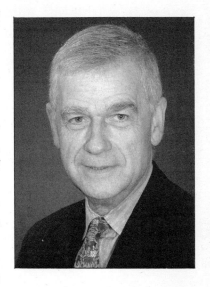

Senator Mark Hatfield of Oregon has been a student, teacher, and practitioner of the American political system for virtually his entire life. A veteran of the Pacific Theater in World War II, he has dedicated his lifetime of public service to preventing and ending armed conflict and improving the human condition.

Hatfield taught political science and was the Dean of Students at his alma mater, Willamette University, before beginning his political career in the Oregon legislature in 1950. In 1956, after terms in both houses of the legislature, he became at the age of 34 the youngest secretary of state in Oregon history. Hatfield was elected governor of Oregon in 1958 and upon reelection in 1962 became the state's first two-term governor in the twentieth century. Hatfield was elected to the U.S. Senate in 1963.

As the ranking Republican on the Senate Appropriations Committee, he has overseen many public-works projects for the Pacific Northwest. The results of his work can be seen in the reforestation of millions of acres of federal lands, Portland's light-rail system, the Bonneville Locks on the Columbia River, and numerous public universities.

Hatfield was born July 12, 1922, in Dallas, Oregon. He has a bachelor of arts degree from Willamette University and a master's degree in political science from Stanford University. He holds more than 80 honorary doctorate degrees. He and his wife, Antoinette, were married in 1958 and have four children and three grandchildren.

ARMED SERVICES
Chairman, Strom Thurmond

Office: (202) 224-5972; fax: (202) 224-1300

Strom Thurmond is serv-
ing his seventh term as
senator from South Car-
olina.

Thurmond was born
December 5, 1902. He
received his bachelor of
arts degree from Clemson
University in 1923. He
served in the U.S. Army
from 1942 to 1946 and was
part of the D-Day invasion
of Normandy. Thurmond
earned 18 military decorations and served a total of
36 years in reserve and active duty.

During his long public service, Thurmond has held the
following positions: South Carolina state senator
(1933–1938), circuit judge for South Carolina (1938–1946),
governor of South Carolina (1947–1951), and U.S. senator
(since 1954).

Thurmond, who began his political career as a Democrat, briefly broke from the party in 1948 to run as the
presidential candidate of the States' Rights Party, receiving
39 electoral votes. He became a Republican in 1964. Thurmond is married to the former Nancy Moore and has four
children, one of whom is deceased.

BANKING, HOUSING, AND URBAN AFFAIRS
Chairman, Alfonse D'Amato

Office: (202) 224-6542; fax: (202) 224-5871

Alfonse D'Amato is currently serving his third term as U.S. senator from New York.

Senator D'Amato champions New York interests through his work on the Senate floor and on the following important committees: Appropriations; Banking, Housing, and Urban Affairs; and Intelligence. In his current role as chairman of the Banking, Housing, and Urban Affairs Committee, he has a decisive impact on legislation affecting the nation's economy. The committee's scope includes small business; housing; transportation; consumer credit; mortgage; commercial lending; the integrity of America's financial institutions; the securities, bond, and commodities markets; and trade and export enhancement.

D'Amato is a vocal critic of government policies and regulations that discourage banks from providing credit to small business and has sponsored legislation to stimulate lending in this key sector. In a related effort, he has advocated legislation to encourage private investment in the nation's inner cities, minority neighborhoods, and other economically distressed areas.

D'Amato, the co-chairman of the International Narcotics Control Caucus and a leader in the fight against illegal drugs, successfully sponsored legislation in 1988 to impose the death penalty on drug kingpins. He strongly supports criminal justice reform, including preventative detention for repeat violent offenders.

A proponent of fair trade, D'Amato has worked to expand open markets abroad for U.S. products and strengthen enforcement against illegal and predatory trade practices by foreign firms.

D'Amato chaired the Helsinki Commission during the 99th Congress and fought for human rights in the former Soviet Union, Eastern Europe, China, and Ireland. He pushed for early recognition of Lithuania and for a peaceful resolution of the Yugoslav crisis. He was also an original supporter of Poland's Solidarity movement and called for an investigation to determine Soviet responsibility for the 1981 assassination attempt on Pope John Paul II.

Born in Brooklyn on August 1, 1937, D'Amato was raised on Long Island, where he still resides. He graduated from Chaminade High School and received his bachelor's degree in business administration and a law degree from Syracuse University. He has four children and five grandchildren.

BUDGET
Chairman, Pete Domenici

Office: (202) 224-6621; fax: (202) 224-7371

Pete Domenici is currently serving his fourth term as U.S. senator from New Mexico.

Now in his third decade in the Senate, Domenici works almost exclusively on budget issues. His genuine frustration with the budget deficits of the 1980s and 1990s has led him to recommend the politically toughest of solutions to reduce them: entitlement cuts, including a cost-of-living adjustment freeze for Social Security recipients and a cap on Medicare and Medicaid costs.

To encourage savings and investment, Domenici has pushed for replacing the current tax code with one that is spending based. Under the proposed plan, taxpayers would be allowed to subtract from their taxable incomes the amount of money they have saved, invested, and used for standard consumption-related expenses such as food, clothing, charitable donations, medical expenses, and certain housing costs.

Domenici was born in 1932 in Albuquerque, New Mexico. He received his bachelor of science from the University of New Mexico and his law degree from the University of Denver. He and his wife, Nancy, have eight children.

Shortly after the Republican takeover of the House and Senate, Domenici said,

> The American people have given the Republicans an opportunity to lead, and I believe we are ready. This election has shown wide support for a number of important Republican ideas and initiatives. Republicans will work to make government smaller, more efficient, and more responsive. We will work to pass legislation prohibiting the unfunded mandates that the federal government heaps upon the states and their citizens. We will work to increase accountability and responsibility in government agencies and repeal burdensome federal regulation. We will work to change our welfare system, to break the cycle of poverty and provide a hand-up, not a hand-out. We will reform our tax system—with an eye toward strengthening our economy and giving hard-working, middle-class Americans tax relief.

COMMERCE, SCIENCE, AND TRANSPORTATION
Chairman, Larry Pressler

Office: (202) 224-5842; fax: (202) 224-1630

Larry Pressler is currently serving his third term as U.S. senator from South Dakota. He served two terms in the U.S. House of Representatives prior to his election to the Senate.

Pressler has long worked to decrease government regulation and open foreign markets to U.S. products. In an effort to aid the U.S. agricultural community, he has lobbied for lower European farm subsidies and convinced Nigeria to lift its ban on wheat imports. Pressler has also worked to open the European Common Market to American products.

Pressler has introduced legislation to restrict unwanted telephone solicitations, set a uniform AM radio stereo standard, and make carjacking a federal crime. He has also played a leading role in the oversight of the mega-mergers in the telecommunications industry and in the Judiciary Committee's role on patent and copyright issues.

Born in Humbolt, South Dakota, in 1942, Pressler received his bachelor of arts degree from the University of South Dakota, his master's degree from the Kennedy School of Government, and his law degree from Harvard. He also attended Oxford as a Rhodes Scholar.

Pressler served the U.S. Army from 1966 to 1968 in Vietnam and became the first veteran of that war to be elected to Congress. He and his wife, Harriet, have one child.

ENERGY AND NATURAL RESOURCES
Chairman, Frank Murkowski

Office: (202) 224-6665; fax: (202) 224-5301

Only the fifth person to represent his state in the Senate, Frank H. Murkowski has served as U.S. senator from Alaska since 1980. He has become one of the Senate's leading experts on energy, natural-resource development, and Asia and the Pacific Rim.

Because of his concerns about resource development and rural jobs, Murkowski has pushed legislation to permit mining in northwest Alaska and guarantee timber supply for dependent communities. Recently, he has focused his efforts on ending the export ban on Alaskan North Slope oil and setting aside part of the *Exxon Valdez* oil-spill settlement to fund long-term ocean research. He has also worked to protect jobs in the fishing industry by helping to lead the fight to ban monofilament drift nets—so-called "curtains of death"—on the high seas. As a member of the Energy and Natural Resources Committee and the Foreign Relations Committee, Murkowski has sought to make Alaska's national parks more accessible to domestic and international tourists.

As the ranking Republican on the East Asian and Pacific Affairs Subcommittee of the Senate Foreign Relations Committee, he has led the fight to force Japan to open its markets to American firms. Murkowski also was a part of the effort to reunite Alaskan Eskimos with their counterparts in the Soviet far east. This lead to the 1988 "friendship flight," which helped break the "Ice Curtain" between the United States and the former Soviet Union.

Murkowski received his bachelor of arts degree from Seattle University in 1955, after which he served in the U.S. Coast Guard. He and his wife, Nancy, have six children and eight grandchildren.

ENVIRONMENT AND PUBLIC WORKS
Chairman, John Chafee

Office: (202) 224-2921; fax: (202) 224-7472

John Chafee is currently serving his fourth term as U.S. senator from Rhode Island.

One of Chafee's priorities as U.S. senator is the protection of natural resources and environmental cleanup. He sponsored major legislation in 1993 to restructure the Clean Water Act and extend through the year 2000 the revolving loan fund for state sewer construction at $2.5 billion per year. The legislation also sought to toughen point and nonpoint source pollution controls and advance the efforts to protect threatened wetlands. Chafee helped secure Senate Environment Committee approval of pending legislation to reauthorize the Safe Drinking Water Act, which includes a $6.6 billion program for states and local governments to finance construction of drinking-water treatment facilities.

Another Chafee priority is the elimination of wasteful federal spending. He sponsored an amendment to the 1990 Farm Bill to phase out the federal honey subsidy, which was costing taxpayers $40–$100 million annually. Another amendment to the 1990 Farm Bill that he sponsored sought to end taxpayer subsidies to wealthy farming conglomerates.

Chafee continues to target farm subsidies and other wasteful governmental programs for elimination. In 1994, he advanced legislation with 76 specific spending cuts that would have reduced the deficit by $109 billion over five years. He sponsored legislation in 1994 to provide for a federal balanced budget amendment and has come out in support of giving the president the line-item veto.

Chafee was born in Providence, Rhode Island, and is a graduate of Yale University and Harvard Law School. He served during World War II in the Marine Corps and was a part of the original invasion forces at Guadalcanal. He and his wife, Virginia, have five children.

FINANCE
Chairman, Bob Packwood

Office: (202) 224-5244; fax: (202) 224-3576

Bob Packwood is currently serving his fifth term as U.S. senator from Oregon.

Packwood was born in 1932. He studied at Willamette University in Salem, Oregon, where he received his bachelor of arts in 1954. He received his law degree from New York University.

Packwood worked as a law clerk to former Chief Justice Harold J. Warner of the Oregon Supreme Court from 1957 to 1958, then practiced law in Portland over the next 10 years.

In 1962 he won election to the Oregon legislature as its youngest member. He served three terms in the legislature before election to the U.S. Senate in 1968 as its youngest member. He has been reelected in 1974, 1980, 1986, and 1992.

As Senate Finance Committee Chairman, Packwood is responsible for national tax policy. His committee also oversees major programs like Medicare, Medicaid, Social Security, trade and tariff legislation, and employee benefits.

Packwood counts among his major achievements the 1986 Tax Reform Act, which stripped away many tax preferences and lowered the top income-tax rate. Senator Packwood has four children.

FOREIGN RELATIONS
Chairman, Jesse Helms

Office: (202) 224-6342; fax: (202) 224-7588

Jesse Helms was first elected as U.S. senator from North Carolina in 1972. He is currently serving his fourth term.

Helms was born in Monroe, North Carolina, on October 18, 1921. He attended the Monroe public schools, Wingate Junior College, and Wake Forest College.

He served in the U.S. Navy from 1942 to 1945. After World War II, he became the city editor of the *Raleigh Times* and, later, director of news and programming for the Tobacco Radio Network and Raleigh radio station WRAL.

Helms served as administrative assistant to Senator Willis Smith from 1951 to 1953 and Senator Alton Lennon in 1953. In 1952, he directed the radio-television division of Senator Richard Russell's campaign for the Democratic Party presidential nomination.

From 1953 to 1960, Helms was executive director of the North Carolina Bankers Association and editor of the *Tarheel Banker*, which under his stewardship became the largest state banking publication in America. From 1960 until his election to the Senate, Helms was executive vice president, vice chairman of the board, and assistant chief executive officer of Capitol Broadcasting Company in Raleigh, North Carolina.

An unflinching conservative, Helm has for years been at the center of many of the Senate's most heated debates, ranging from funding for the National Endowment of the Arts to school prayer and abortion. As the new chairman of the Foreign Relations Committee he squared off with President Clinton early, questioning the president's fitness to be commander-in-chief. Helms is married to the former Dorothy Jane Coble of Raleigh and is the father of three children.

GOVERNMENTAL AFFAIRS
Chairman, William Roth

Office: (202) 224-2441; fax: (202) 224-2805

William Roth was first elected to the U.S. Senate from Delaware in 1970 and is currently serving his fifth term.

Roth earned his bachelor of arts from the University of Oregon and his master's in business administration and law degree from Harvard University. He served in the U.S. Army during World War II. Before his election to the Senate Roth was a member of the U.S. House of Representatives and the chairman of the Delaware State Republican Committee.

He is perhaps best known for his co-sponsorship of the Kemp-Roth tax-cut proposal in the late 1970s. The plan, which called for broad-based tax-rate reductions, became the centerpiece of the Reagan supply-side economics agenda in the early 1980s.

Roth was born in 1921 in Great Falls, Montana. He is married to the former Jane Richards and has three children.

JUDICIARY
Chairman, Orrin Hatch

Office: (202) 224-5251; fax: (202) 224-6331

Orrin Hatch is currently serving his fourth term as U.S. senator from Utah.

During his years as ranking Republican on the Senate Judiciary Committee, Hatch pushed for constitutional amendments to allow silent prayer and require a balanced budget. He has been a leader in the fight for tougher crime laws and supported legislation that reestablished the federal death penalty. He has led the movement for habeas corpus reform, which seeks to establish reasonable limits to the number of appeals available to convicted criminals. Hatch also played a key role in the passage of the Hate Crimes Statistics Act.

Other issues that Hatch has focused on include legislation that allows the elderly to receive medical care at home if they choose; his Omnibus Health Act, which ensures the availability of needed vaccines for children; and the Job Training Partnership Act and the Carl Perkins Vocational Education Act, which help adolescents and unemployed adults obtain job skills and education. Hatch has also consistently fought against new government mandates that would severely damage small business as well as deny freedom to workers to negotiate their own pay and benefits.

Hatch received his bachelor of science in history from Brigham Young University and his law degree from the University of Pittsburgh. He is married to the former Elaine Hansen and has six children and fifteen grandchildren.

Analyzing Hatch's elevation to the chairmanship of the Senate Judiciary Committee, the *New York Times* noted that "Although Mr. Hatch's conservative credentials are undisputed, administration officials and Republican colleagues expect that he will be less confrontational with the White House than Jesse Helms."

LABOR AND HUMAN RESOURCES
Chairwoman, Nancy Kassebaum

Office: (202) 224-4774; fax: (202) 224-3514

Nancy Landon Kassebaum is currently serving her third term as U.S. senator from Kansas.

Kassebaum has sought to make states more responsible for governing by turning over to them power that has traditionally resided in Washington. She supports, for example, shifting all responsibility for providing welfare to the states and believes that the Occupational Safety and Health Administration needlessly duplicates the work of state-level programs.

Kassebaum has said her first priority in the Labor and Human Resources Committee is downsizing. She has already initiated a review of hundreds of federal job-training programs that cost taxpayers billions of dollars each year. She has promised to consider cuts in such federal programs as the National Endowment of the Arts, the National Science Foundation, the Public Health Service, and the National Institutes of Health.

Kassebaum is the daughter of Alfred M. Landon, the 1936 Republican presidential candidate. She received her bachelor of arts from the University of Kansas and her master's from the University of Michigan. She has four children.

RULES AND ADMINISTRATION
Chairman, Ted Stevens

Office: (202) 224-3004 fax: (202) 224-1044

Ted Stevens is serving his fifth term as U.S. senator from Alaska, having first been elected in 1968.

Stevens has long been a supporter of managed use of natural resources in Alaska and the rest of the United States. In response to the *Exxon Valdez* oil spill in Prince William Sound, he championed legislation aimed at helping the resources of the area to recover.

Stevens has fought to protect the fisheries of Alaska, ban the use of "invisible" monofilament nets in the high seas, stop the overfishing of international waters, and ratify the International Salmon Treaty. To make America less dependent on foreign sources of energy, Stevens has called for oil exploration in the Arctic National Wildlife refugee.

Born in Indianapolis, Indiana, Stevens has been an Alaskan since the early 1950s. A graduate of the University of California at Los Angeles and Harvard Law School, he served as U.S. attorney in Fairbanks, Alaska. Before coming to Washington, he served two terms in the Alaska legislature, where he was majority leader and speaker pro tem.

During World War II, Stevens was a pilot with the 14th Air Force in China, the Flying Tigers. In the Eisenhower administration, he was assistant to the Secretary of the Interior and solicitor of the Interior Department.

He and his wife, Catherine, have one child. Senator Stevens has five children by his first wife, Ann, now deceased.

SMALL BUSINESS
Chairman, Christopher Bond

Office: (202) 224-5721; fax: (202) 224-8149

Christopher "Kit" Bond is serving his second term as U.S. senator from Missouri. He was originally elected in 1986.

Bond was born March 6, 1939. He received his bachelor's degree from Princeton University and his law degree from the University of Virginia.

After serving a year as Missouri's assistant attorney general, Bond ran successfully for state auditor in 1970. Two years later, at age 33, he was elected governor of Missouri, becoming the youngest governor in the state's history. He reclaimed his seat in 1980 after suffering a defeat in 1976.

In December 1994, Bond was named by the new Republican majority to lead the regulatory-reform effort in the Senate. He and Texas Senator Kay Bailey Hutchinson were named as co-chairpersons for the Senate Republican Relief Task Force.

"Overly burdensome federal regulations are an enormous strain on our economy," Bond said. "Especially hard hit are small businesses and entrepreneurs who find the costs of compliance with existing regulations excessive and unworkable. Conservative estimates place the cost of regulation at over $500 billion annually, or about an average of $5,000 per household each year. Instead of providing incentives for America's small-business owners, the government promotes an anticompetitive environment that strangles job creation."

He and his wife, Carolyn, have one child.

VETERANS AFFAIRS
Chairman, Alan Simpson

Office: (202) 224-3424; fax: (202) 224-1315

Alan Simpson is currently serving his third term as U.S. senator from Wyoming. He will be up for reelection in 1996.

Simpson's folksy manner and his reputation for plain speaking have made him a nationally known figure. Although he is a conservative from a conservative state, his work on major legislation such as immigration reform won respect from both sides of the aisle. He was mentioned as a possible George Bush running mate in the presidential campaign of 1988 but pulled himself out of the running.

Simpson is the son of former Wyoming Governor and Senator Milward Simpson. He worked as a trial lawyer and served in the Wyoming state legislature before his election to the Senate. Born in 1931, Senator Simpson earned his bachelor of science and law degree from the University of Wyoming.

SENATE SELECT COMMITTEES

ETHICS
Chairman, Mitch McConnell

Office: (202) 224-2541; fax: (202) 224-2499

Mitch McConnell was first elected as U.S. senator from Kentucky in 1984 and is now serving his second term.

Born in 1942, McConnell was educated at the University of Louisville and the University of Kentucky School of Law. Before his election to the Senate, he served as a county judge, a deputy assistant attorney general, and as chief legislative assistant to former Kentucky Senator Marlow Cook.

McConnell has earned a reputation as a solid conservative, focusing on issues such as stopping public financing of elections, capping contingency fees for trial lawyers, and fighting child pornography.

INDIAN AFFAIRS
Chairman, Thad Cochran

Office: (202) 224-5054; fax: (202) 224-9450

Thad Cochran was first elected as U.S. senator from Mississippi in 1978; he is currently serving his third term. Born in 1937, Cochran was educated at the University of Mississippi, where he received his bachelor of arts and law degree.

Prior to serving in the Senate, Cochran was a member of the U.S. House of Representatives from 1972 to 1978 and, before that, a practicing attorney.

Although Cochran has a consistently conservative voting record, he has not sought to champion right-wing causes in a rancorous or divisive fashion. His work has focused on farm legislation, education and training, and support for science and technology.

INTELLIGENCE
Chairman, Arlen Specter

Office: (202) 224-4254; fax: (202) 224-9029

Arlen Specter is currently serving his third term as a U.S. senator from Pennsylvania.

Senator Specter has spent a substantial portion of his career focused on intelligence and investigative issues. His first foray into the limelight was in 1964 as a member of the Warren Commission, which investigated the Kennedy assassination. In the Senate, he authored the Terrorist Prosecution Act, a tough anti-terrorism bill. He also authored legislation creating the position of inspector general within the Central Intelligence Agency. This was the only reform legislation that came out of the Iran-Contra hearings.

Specter has also highlighted public safety. His Armed Career Criminal Act of 1984, which was expanded in 1986, makes it a federal offense with a mandatory 15-years-to-life sentence for a career criminal found in possession of a firearm. He crafted the Missing Children's Assistance Act and is responsible for tough new laws against child pornography.

Born in 1930, Specter received his bachelor of arts from the University of Pennsylvania and his law degree from Yale University. He served in the U.S. Air Force from

1951 to 1953. He is married to the former Joan Levy and has two children.

Recently, Senator Specter announced that he is exploring the possibility of seeking the 1996 Republican presidential nomination as a centrist candidate.

SPECIAL COMMITTEE ON AGING
Chairman, William Cohen

Office: (202) 224-2523; fax: (202) 224-2693

William Cohen is currently serving his third term as a U.S. senator from Maine.

Much of Cohen's legislative work has focused on the health-care industry. He has come out in favor of penalizing doctors and other health-care providers who overcharge Medicare and punishing drug companies whose prices rise faster than inflation. He has proposed a nationwide, low-cost health-care plan that gives individuals basic coverage and includes tax credit for health insurance premiums

Military issues have also been at the center of Cohen's legislative agenda. He supported the Reagan military buildup of the 1980s and has opposed the Clinton cuts, which he feels have harmed national security.

Cohen was born in 1940. He received his bachelor of arts from Bowdoin College and his law degree from Boston University. An avid writer, Cohen has published a volume of poetry and a mystery novel. He has two children.

CHAPTER FIVE

KEEPING SCORE AND TALKING BACK

Talk back to the men and women who represent you in Washington. Tell them how you feel about the issues that touch the lives of you and your loved ones. Get involved in the workings of government, in the passionate debates of new ideas and old values. Here is how you can do it.

HOW TO CONTACT THE NEW CONGRESS

Calling

You can reach the office of any member of Congress by calling the U.S. Capitol at 202-224-3121. Simply tell the operator the name of the senator or representative you wish to contact. (See the Appendix for a complete list of members by state and district. The phone numbers for the new leaders and chairmen of the 104th Congress are listed separately at the beginning of their profiles in Chapters 3 and 4.)

Because of the sheer volume of calls that flood daily into Congressional offices, don't expect to speak directly to your senator or representative. Most likely your call will be taken be a staff member who nonetheless will probably be able to respond to your questions and concerns or direct you to someone who can.

A few tips when calling a Congressional office:

- Make it clear that you are a constituent—it adds weight to your call.

- Be sure to express your views about particular bills and issues. Congressional offices maintain informal opinion polls to track the mood of constituents.

- If you wish to discuss an issue in greater detail, ask to speak to the staff member to whom it has been assigned.

Your representative is likely to have a district office in or near your community. You can find out by checking the government pages in the phone book. Most members of Congress and their staffs prefer that you call the district offices, which are set up primarily to handle constituent problems. Staff members in local offices are more accustomed to dealing with community issues than their Washington counterparts, whose focus is more national in scope.

Writing

Letters to Congressional offices should be brief and clear; thoughts and opinions are best expressed when honed into concise sentences.

When writing a member of the House or Senate, use the following forms of address (no room number or street address is needed):

> The Honorable Georgia Hughes
> United States Senate
> Washington, D.C. 20510

> Dear Senator Hughes:

> The Honorable Roger Stewart
> United States House of Representatives
> Washington, D.C. 20515

> Dear Representative Stewart:

Where available, fax numbers for the new Congressional leaders are included at the beginning of their respective profiles in Chapters 3 and 4.

Can You Make a Difference?

Are your phone calls heard and your letters and faxes read? Do they matter? Be assured—they most certainly do. Although you may get the impression that your message is not receiving individual attention from your representative, records are kept and your views do register in the minds of members and key staff. After all, your representatives are always only an election away from becoming private citizens.

The leaders of the 104th Congress have expressed a determination not to repeat what they view as the isolation and arrogance of those who preceded them. They say that lessons have been learned. If this is the case, then you can likely expect your views to matter more than ever.

THE CITIZEN'S SCORECARD

House Republicans have promised a frenzy of internal Congressional reform as well as dramatic shifts in national policies—all in the first 100 days of the new Congress. Will they keep their promises? Will the president go along? Or, will gridlock once again reign supreme?

Republican Contract Promises

PROMISE	PROMISE KEPT	PROMISE BROKEN
Congressional Reforms		
Apply all laws to Congress	❑	❑
Cut number of committees	❑	❑
Cut committee staffs by one-third	❑	❑
Limit terms of committee chairs	❑	❑
Ban proxy voting in committee	❑	❑
Implement honest numbers budget with zero baseline	❑	❑
Require three-fifths majority to pass tax increase	❑	❑
Comprehensive audit of House funds	❑	❑

*Not required for Congressional reforms

Hold your elected officials accountable for the promises they've made! Use the following Citizen's Scorecard to keep track of their progress. (For more information on promises listed below, consult the "Fine Print" section of Chapter 2.)

PRESIDENTIAL ACTION S (SIGNED) V (VETOED)	HOW MY REPRESENTATIVES VOTED (YES/NO)		
	Sen.	Sen.	Rep.
*	___	___	___
*	___	___	___
*	___	___	___
*	___	___	___
*	___	___	___
*	___	___	___
*	___	___	___
*	___	___	___

PROMISE	PROMISE KEPT	PROMISE BROKEN
The Fiscal Responsibility Act		
Pass Constitutional amendment to balance the budget	❏	❏
Enact line-item veto	❏	❏
Taking Back Our Streets Act		
Limit death penalty appeals	❏	❏
Ten-year mandatory sentence for using gun in the commission of a felony	❏	❏
Mandatory victim restitution	❏	❏
$10 billion law enforcement block grants	❏	❏
Require state truth-in-sentencing in exchange for prison funds	❏	❏
Reform "exclusionary rule"	❏	❏
Stop abusive prisoner lawsuits	❏	❏
Deport criminal aliens	❏	❏
The Personal Responsibility Act		
Terminate AFDC after 2 years for some, 5 years for all	❏	❏
Give states option of ending AFDC for teen mothers	❏	❏
Require work for welfare	❏	❏
Cap welfare spending	❏	❏

	HOW MY		
	REPRESENTATIVES VOTED		
PRESIDENTIAL ACTION	(YES/NO)		
S (SIGNED) **V** (VETOED)	**Sen.**	**Sen.**	**Rep.**
S V	___	___	___
S V	___	___	___
S V	___	___	___
S V	___	___	___
S V	___	___	___
S V	___	___	___
S V	___	___	___
S V	___	___	___
S V	___	___	___
S V	___	___	___
S V	___	___	___
S V	___	___	___
S V	___	___	___
S V	___	___	___

PROMISE	PROMISE KEPT	PROMISE BROKEN
Turn welfare over to the states with block grants	❏	❏
Increase child-support enforcement	❏	❏
Tougher penalties for child pornography and sex crimes	❏	❏
$500 dependent-care tax credit for families caring for elderly parent	❏	❏
The American Dream Restoration Act		
$500-per-child tax credit for families earning up to $200,000	❏	❏
Reform anti-marriage tax penalty	❏	❏
Create American Dream Savings Accounts with up to $2,000 per year of IRA-like tax benefits	❏	❏
The National Security Restoration Act		
Restrict U.N. command of U.S. troops	❏	❏
Commission study of defense needs and readiness	❏	❏
Increase defense spending	❏	❏
Renewed commitment to missile defense system	❏	❏
Expansion of NATO membership	❏	❏

PRESIDENTIAL ACTION	HOW MY REPRESENTATIVES VOTED (YES/NO)		
S (SIGNED) V (VETOED)	Sen.	Sen.	Rep.
S V	___	___	___
S V	___	___	___
S V	___	___	___
S V	___	___	___
S V	___	___	___
S V	___	___	___
S V	___	___	___
S V	___	___	___
S V	___	___	___
S V	___	___	___
S V	___	___	___
S V	___	___	___

PROMISE	PROMISE KEPT	PROMISE BROKEN
Senior Citizen Equity Act		
Increase social security earning-limit threshold to $30,000 over 5 years	❏	❏
Lower amount of social security benefits subject to taxation from 85% to 50%	❏	❏
Create tax incentives for those buying private long-term-care insurance	❏	❏
Allow housing communities with 80% senior residents to use Fair Housing legal standards	❏	❏
Job Creation and Wage Enhancement Act		
Cut the capital-gains tax	❏	❏
Allow businesses to depreciate 100% of their investments	❏	❏
Allow small businesses to deduct the first $25,000 they invest in equipment and inventory	❏	❏
Clarify home-office deduction		
Increase estate tax exemption from $600,000 to $750,000	❏	❏
Allow taxpayers to designate 10% of taxes to deficit reduction	❏	❏
Require risk assessment/cost-benefit analysis for new regulations	❏	❏

PRESIDENTIAL ACTION S (SIGNED) V (VETOED)		HOW MY REPRESENTATIVES VOTED (YES/NO)		
		Sen.	Sen.	Rep.
S	V	___	___	___
S	V	___	___	___
S	V	___	___	___
S	V	___	___	___
S	V	___	___	___
S	V	___	___	___
S	V	___	___	___
S	V	___	___	___
S	V	___	___	___
S	V	___	___	___

PROMISE	PROMISE KEPT	PROMISE BROKEN
Create regulatory budget to expose costs of compliance	❏	❏
Void future laws that impose unfunded mandates on states and localities	❏	❏
Strengthen Paperwork Reduction Act	❏	❏
Provide compensation for private-property takings	❏	❏
Require regulatory-impact analysis	❏	❏
The Commonsense Legal Reforms Act		
Enact loser-pays provision to discourage frivolous lawsuits	❏	❏
Prevent use of "junk science" in court testimony	❏	❏
Put reasonable limits on punitive damage awards	❏	❏
Require attorneys to divulge fees up front	❏	❏
Require clearer legislation to prevent need for lawsuits	❏	❏
Apportion liability on basis of responsibility, not deep pockets	❏	❏
Term Limits		
Pass term limits of either (a) 6 years for representatives and 12 for senators, or (b) 12 years for both	❏	❏

PRESIDENTIAL ACTION		HOW MY REPRESENTATIVES VOTED (YES/NO)		
S (SIGNED)	V (VETOED)	Sen.	Sen.	Rep.
S	V	___	___	___
S	V	___	___	___
S	V	___	___	___
S	V	___	___	___
S	V	___	___	___
S	V	___	___	___
S	V	___	___	___
S	V	___	___	___
S	V	___	___	___
S	V	___	___	___
S	V	___	___	___
S	V	___	___	___

CHAPTER SIX

A CHALLENGE FOR THE AMERICAN PEOPLE

Do You Really Mean It?

Many Americans are fond of complaining that, regardless of party, once our elected officials get into office, they quickly forsake their promises and forget for whom they work. But suppose we elected a Congress that actually does what it promised and delivers major reductions in government programs, some of which we personally favor and from which we personally benefit?

If the early record of performance is any guide, we have indeed elected that kind of Congress!

Furthermore, at least for the time being, Speaker Gingrich and his fellow Republicans are in full command of the political and policy agenda, prompting President Clinton and many other Democrats to join in the rush to cut taxes and eliminate or reduce government programs and regulations. It is very likely that many items on the Republican agenda will pass Congress by a wide margin. Some may even be signed into law by President Clinton!

So now it is our rhetoric and resolve that will be put to the test. For years, many of us have been complaining about the burden of government spending and regulation, the intrusion of Big Brother into our lives, and the exploding deficits and spiraling national debt. But how many of us have stepped willingly up to the plate and said, "Yes, Congress, go right ahead and cut the programs that benefit me. It will be better for our country and in the long run perhaps even better for me if you do." As we demand that government get its hand out of our pocket, how many of us are truly prepared to take our hands out of the government's deep pocket?

Economist Robert Samuelson recently cited statistics showing that 52 percent of all American families receive some type of government transfer payment—ranging from social security to food stamps to veterans benefits. Still more benefit from programs such as farm subsidies. Analyzing this startling fact in the context of the Republican Contract with America, Samuelson wrote before the election:

> The myth of the Right is that conservatives want to dismantle Big Government. But no one on the Right proposes sweeping cutbacks of government. "Conservatives may attack this or that ridiculous feature of overweaning government," writes David Frum in his book *Dead Right*, but radical criticism of the very idea that "Washington should . . . redistribute one quarter of the nation's wealth has simply petered out."

And why not? Radical retrenchment might alienate millions of voters. . . .

As a campaign document, the "contract" may or may not succeed. But as a governing blueprint, it fails because it panders to popular inconsistency. Americans are hopelessly dependent on Big Government and rapidly contemptuous of it. (*Newsweek*, October 24, 1994)

From the perspective of the Right, columnist George Will probed this issue as well and put it squarely on the table in a post-election November 13, 1994, exchange with Rep. Newt Gingrich on ABC News' "This Week with David Brinkley":

Gingrich: I think we ought to have an open dialogue about whether the American people want to go through that transformation to a smaller government, or whether they want to continue to borrow from their children and grandchildren. That's a legitimate dialogue.

Will: That is the question, isn't it? Whether the American people are ideologically conservative but operationally liberal, that they will flinch when it comes time to cut. Let me give you a few examples. One of the largest expansions of the government's regulatory and intrusive activity in recent years was the Americans with Disabilities Act. Will the Republican majorities prune that legislation?

Gingrich: I don't think we'll—again, I want to draw a distinction between more, less, and transformation, George. I believe that local communities should have the opportunity to apply local common sense without a Washington bureaucracy. You want to maximize every American's right to participate fully. You want to maximize those with challenges and disabilities. . . .

Will: Let me ask about agriculture subsidies. Stern critics of agriculture subsidies include Dick Armey in the House, Phil Gramm in the Senate. Fervent defenders of agriculture subsidies include Bob Dole. Are the Republicans seriously going to prune agriculture subsidies?

Gingrich: I think the Republicans are going to seriously look at how do you, over the next five to seven years, make a transition in agriculture, recognizing that one of our major problems is the degree to which the European Common Market subsidizes its agricultural producers and puts American producers at a significant disadvantage in the world market. . . .

Will: I may be wrong, but I think I'm hearing that agriculture subsidies are only going to be looked at and that the Americans with Disabilities Act is pretty safe.

The American Trucking Associations' Tom Donohue has observed, "Somehow the *next* revolution has to be people coming to understand that you can't have it both ways." To use George Will's terms, we can't be both ideologically conservative and operationally liberal at once without consigning our nation to still more gridlock, drift, and dangerous contradictions in policy that smother free enterprise through exploding deficits or excessive government control.

We sent a new Congress to Washington to fundamentally alter the role of government in our lives—to restore individual liberty and personal responsibility as core values in our society, and to reconnect American democracy to the principle of limited government. If this Congress fails us, we can replace it in the next election. But if we whine and complain and take exception as Congress strives to make good on the task we asked it to perform, who is failing whom?

The challenge facing Americans is to be as bold as the dream we empowered through our votes on November 8, 1994.

MEMBERS OF THE 104TH CONGRESS

ALABAMA

Senate

Richard Shelby (Rep.)
Howell Heflin (Dem.)

House

1st	Sonny Callahan (Rep.)
2nd	Terry Everett (Rep.)
3rd	Glen Browder (Dem.)
4th	Tom Bevill (Dem.)
5th	Robert E. (Bud) Cramer, Jr. (Dem.)
6th	Spencer Bachus (Rep.)
7th	Earl F. Hilliard (Dem.)

ALASKA

Senate

Frank H. Murkowski (Rep.)
Ted Stevens (Rep.)

House

At large: Don Young (Rep.)

ARIZONA

Senate

Jon L. Kyl (Rep.)
John McCain (Rep.)

House

1st	Matt Salmon (Rep.)
2nd	Ed Pastor (Dem.)
3rd	Bob Stump (Rep.)
4th	John Shadegg (Rep.)
5th	Jim Kolbe (Rep.)
6th	J. D. Hayworth (Rep.)

ARKANSAS

Senate

Dale Bumpers (Dem.)
David Pryor (Dem.)

House

1st	Blanche M. Lambert (Dem.)
2nd	Ray Thornton (Dem.)
3rd	Tim W. Hutchinson (Rep.)
4th	Jay Dickey (Rep.)

CALIFORNIA

Senate

Barbara Boxer (Dem.)
Dianne Feinstein (Dem.)

House

1st	Frank Riggs (Rep.)
2nd	Wally Herger (Rep.)
3rd	Vic Fazio (Dem.)
4th	John T. Doolittle (Rep.)
5th	Robert T. Matsui (Dem.)
6th	Lynn C. Wolsey (Dem.)
7th	George Miller (Dem.)
8th	Nancy Pelosi (Dem.)
9th	Ronald V. Dellums (Dem.)
10th	Bill Baker (Rep.)
11th	Richard W. Pombo (Rep.)
12th	Tom Lantos (Dem.)
13th	Fortney (Pete) Stark (Dem.)
14th	Anna G. Eshoo (Dem.)
15th	Norman Y. Mineta (Dem.)
16th	Zoe Lofgren (Dem.)
17th	Sam Farr (Dem.)
18th	Gary A. Condit (Dem.)
19th	George P. Randanovich (Rep.)
20th	Calvin M. Dooley (Dem.)
21st	William M. Thomas (Rep.)
22nd	Andrea Seastrand (Rep.)
23rd	Elton Gallegly (Rep.)
24th	Anthony Beilenson (Dem.)
25th	Howard P. (Buck) McKeon (Rep.)
26th	Howard L. Berman (Dem.)
27th	Carlos J. Moorhead (Rep.)
28th	David Dreier (Rep.)

29th	Henry A. Waxman (Dem.)
30th	Xavier Becerra (Dem.)
31st	Matthew G. Martinez (Dem.)
32nd	Julian C. Dixon (Dem.)
33rd	Lucille Roybal-Allard (Dem.)
34th	Esteban Edward Torres (Dem.)
35th	Maxine Waters (Dem.)
36th	Jane Harman (Dem.)
37th	Walter R. Tucker III (Dem.)
38th	Steve Horn (Rep.)
39th	Edward R. Royce (Rep.)
40th	Jerry Lewis (Rep.)
41st	Jay Kim (Rep.)
42nd	George E. Brown, Jr. (Dem.)
43rd	Ken Calvert (Rep.)
44th	Sonny Bono (Rep.)
45th	Dana Rohrabacher (Rep.)
46th	Robert K. Dornan (Rep.)
47th	Christopher Cox (Rep.)
48th	Ron Packard (Rep.)
49th	Brian P. Bilbray (Rep.)
50th	Bob Filner (Dem.)
51st	Randy (Duke) Cunningham (Rep.)
52nd	Duncan Hunter (Rep.)

COLORADO

Senate

Hank Brown (Rep.)
Ben Nighthorse Campbell (Dem.)

House

1st	Patricia Schroeder (Dem.)
2nd	David E. Skaggs (Dem.)

3rd	Scott McInnis (Rep.)
4th	Wayne Allard (Rep.)
5th	Joel Hefley (Rep.)
6th	Dan Schaefer (Rep.)

CONNECTICUT

Senate
Christopher J. Dodd (Dem.)
Joseph I. Lieberman (Dem.)

House

1st	Barbara B. Kennelly (Dem.)
2nd	Sam Gejdenson (Dem.)
3rd	Rosa L. DeLauro (Dem.)
4th	Christopher Shays (Rep.)
5th	Gary A. Franks (Rep.)
6th	Nancy L. Johnson (Rep.)

DELAWARE

Senate
Joseph R. Biden (Dem.)
William V. Roth (Rep.)

House
At large: Michael N. Castle (Rep.)

FLORIDA

Senate
Bob Graham (Dem.)
Connie Mack (Rep.)

House

1st	Joe Scarborough (Rep.)
2nd	Pete Peterson (Dem.)
3rd	Corrine Brown (Dem.)
4th	Tillie K. Fowler (Rep.)
5th	Karen L. Thurman (Dem.)
6th	Cliff Stearns (Rep.)
7th	John L. Mica (Rep.)
8th	Bill McCollum (Rep.)
9th	Michael Bilirakis (Rep.)
10th	C. W. Bill Young (Rep.)
11th	Sam Gibbons (Dem.)
12th	Charles T. Canady (Rep.)
13th	Dan Miller (Rep.)
14th	Porter J. Goss (Rep.)
15th	Dave Weldon (Rep.)
16th	Mark Foley (Rep.)
17th	Carrie P. Meek (Dem.)
18th	Ileana Ros-Lehtinen (Rep.)
19th	Harry Johnston (Dem.)
20th	Peter Deustch (Dem.)
21st	Lincoln Diaz-Balart (Rep.)
22nd	E. Clay Shaw, Jr. (Rep.)
23rd	Alcee L. Hastings (Dem.)

GEORGIA

Senate

Paul Coverdell (Rep.)
Sam Nunn (Dem.)

House

1st	Jack Kingston (Rep.)
2nd	Sanford D. Bishop (Dem.)

3rd	Mac Collins (Rep.)
4th	John Linder (Rep.)
5th	John Lewis (Dem.)
6th	Newt Gingrich (Rep.)
7th	Bob Barr (Rep.)
8th	Saxby Chambliss (Rep.)
9th	Nathan Deal (Dem.)
10th	Charlie Norwood (Rep.)
11th	Cynthia A. McKinney (Dem.)

HAWAII

Senate

Daniel Akaka (Dem.)
Daniel Inouye (Dem.)

House

1st	Neil Abercrombie (Dem.)
2nd	Patsy T. Mink (Dem.)

IDAHO

Senate

Larry E. Craig (Rep.)
Dirk Kempthorne (Rep.)

House

1st	Helen Chenoweth (Rep.)
2nd	Michael D. Crapo (Rep.)

ILLINOIS

Senate

Carol Moseley-Braun (Dem.)
Paul Simon (Dem.)

House

1st	Bobby L. Rush (Dem.)
2nd	Mel Reynolds (Dem.)
3rd	William O. Lipinski (Dem.)
4th	Luis V. Gutierrez (Dem.)
5th	Michael Patrick Flanagan (Rep.)
6th	Henry J. Hyde (Rep.)
7th	Cardiss Collins (Dem.)
8th	Philip M. Crane (Rep.)
9th	Sidney R. Yates (Dem.)
10th	John Edward Porter (Rep.)
11th	Gerald C. (Jerry) Weller (Rep.)
12th	Jerry F. Costello (Dem.)
13th	Harris W. Fawell (Rep.)
14th	John Dennis Hastert (Rep.)
15th	Thomas W. Ewing (Rep.)
16th	Donald A. Manzullo (Rep.)
17th	Lane Evans (Dem.)
18th	Ray LaHood (Rep.)
19th	Glenn Poshard (Dem.)
20th	Richard J. Durbin (Dem.)

INDIANA

Senate

Daniel R. Coats (Rep.)
Richard G. Lugar (Rep.)

House

1st	Peter J. Visclosky (Dem.)
2nd	David M. McIntosh (Rep.)
3rd	Tim Roemer (Dem.)
4th	Mark Edward Souder (Rep.)
5th	Stephen E. Buyer (Rep.)
6th	Dan Burton (Rep.)
7th	John T. Myers (Rep.)
8th	John Hostettler (Rep.)
9th	Lee H. Hamilton (Dem.)
10th	Andrew Jacobs, Jr. (Dem.)

IOWA

Senate

Charles E. Grassley (Rep.)
Tom Harkin (Dem.)

House

1st	James A. Leach (Rep.)
2nd	Jim Nussle (Rep.)
3rd	Jim Lightfoot (Rep.)
4th	Greg Ganske (Rep.)
5th	Tom Latham (Rep.)

KANSAS

Senate

Robert Dole (Rep.)
Nancy Kassebaum (Rep.)

House

1st	Pat Roberts (Rep.)
2nd	Sam Brownback (Rep.)

3rd   Jan Meyers (Rep.)
4th   Todd Tiahrt (Rep.)

KENTUCKY

Senate

Wendell H. Ford (Dem.)
Mitch McConnell (Rep.)

House

1st   Edward Whitfield (Rep.)
2nd   Ron Lewis (Rep.)
3rd   Mike Ward (Dem.)
4th   Jim Bunning (Rep.)
5th   Harold Rogers (Rep.)
6th   Scotty Baesler (Dem.)

LOUISIANA

Senate

John Breaux (Dem.)
J. Bennett Johnston (Dem.)

House

1st   Bob Livingston (Rep.)
2nd   William J. Jefferson (Dem.)
3rd   W. J. (Billy) Tauzin (Dem.)
4th.   Cleo Fields (Dem.)
5th   Jim McCrery (Rep.)
6th   Richard H. Baker (Rep.)
7th   James A. Hayes (Dem.)

MAINE

Senate
Olympia Snowe (Rep.)
William S. Cohen (Rep.)

House
1st	James B. Longley, Jr. (Rep.)
2nd	John Baldacci (Dem.)

MARYLAND

Senate
Barbara A. Mikulski (Dem.)
Paul S. Sarbanes (Dem.)

House
1st	Wayne T. Gilchrest (Rep.)
2nd	Robert L. Ehrlich, Jr. (Rep.)
3rd	Benjamin Cardin (Dem.)
4th	Albert Russell Wynn (Dem.)
5th	Steny H. Hoyer (Dem.)
6th	Roscoe G. Bartlett (Rep.)
7th	Kweisi Mfume (Dem.)
8th	Constance A. Morella (Rep.)

MASSACHUSETTS

Senate
Edward M. Kennedy (Dem.)
John F. Kerry (Dem.)

House

1st	John W. Olver (Dem.)
2nd	Richard E. Neal (Dem.)
3rd	Peter Blute (Rep.)
4th	Barney Frank (Dem.)
5th	Martin T. Meehan (Dem.)
6th	Peter G. Torkildsen (Rep.)
7th	Edward J. Markey (Dem.)
8th	Joseph P. Kennedy II (Dem.)
9th	John Joseph Moakley (Dem.)
10th	Gerry E. Studds (Dem.)

MICHIGAN

Senate

Spencer Abraham (Rep.)
Carl Levin (Dem.)

House

1st	Bart Stupak (Dem.)
2nd	Peter Hoekstra (Rep.)
3rd	Vernon J. Ehlers (Rep.)
4th	Dave Camp (Rep.)
5th	James A. Barcia (Dem.)
6th	Fred Upton (Rep.)
7th	Nick Smith (Rep.)
8th	Dick Chrysler (Rep.)
9th	Dale E. Kildee (Dem.)
10th	David E. Bonior (Dem.)
11th	Joe Knollenberg (Rep.)
12th	Sander M. Levin (Dem.)
13th	Lynn Nancy Rivers (Dem.)
14th	John Conyers, Jr. (Dem.)
15th	Barbara-Rose Collins (Dem.)
16th	John D. Dingell (Dem.)

MINNESOTA

Senate
Rodney D. Grams (Rep.)
Paul Wellstone (Dem.)

House
1st	Gil Gutknecht (Rep.)
2nd	David Minge (Dem.)
3rd	Jim Ramstad (Rep.)
4th	Bruce F. Vento (Dem.)
5th	Martin Olav Sabo (Dem.)
6th	William P. (Bill) Luther (Dem.)
7th	Collin C. Peterson (Dem.)
8th	James L. Oberstar (Dem.)

MISSISSIPPI

Senate
Thad Cochran (Rep.)
Trent Lott (Rep.)

House
1st	Roger Wicker (Rep.)
2nd	Bernie G. Thompson (Dem.)
3rd	G. V. (Sonny) Montgomery (Dem.)
4th	Mike Parker (Dem.)
5th	Gene Taylor (Dem.)

MISSOURI

Senate
John Ashcroft (Rep.)
Christopher S. (Kit) Bond (Rep.)

House

1st	William (Bill) Clay (Dem.)
2nd	James M. Talent (Rep.)
3rd	Richard A. Gephardt (Dem.)
4th	Ike Skelton (Dem.)
5th	Karen McCarthy (Dem.)
6th	Pat Danner (Dem.)
7th	Mel Hancock (Rep.)
8th	Bill Emerson (Rep.)
9th	Harold L. Volkmer (Dem.)

MONTANA

Senate

Max S. Baucus (Dem.)
Conrad Burns (Rep.)

House

At large: Pat Williams (Dem.)

NEBRASKA

Senate

J. James Exon (Dem.)
Robert Kerrey (Dem.)

House

1st	Doug Bereuter (Rep.)
2nd	Jon Christensen (Rep.)
3rd	Bill Barrett (Rep.)

NEVADA

Senate

Richard Bryan (Dem.)
Harry Reid (Dem.)

House

1st	John Ensign (Rep.)
2nd	Barbara F. Vucanovich (Rep.)

NEW HAMPSHIRE

Senate

Judd Gregg (Rep.)
Robert C. (Bob) Smith (Rep.)

House

1st	William H. Zeliff, Jr. (Rep.)
2nd	Charles Bass (Rep.)

NEW JERSEY

Senate

Bill Bradley (Dem.)
Frank Lautenberg (Dem.)

House

1st	Robert E. Andrews (Dem.)
2nd	Frank A. LoBiondo (Rep.)
3rd	Jim Saxton (Rep.)
4th	Christopher H. Smith (Rep.)
5th	Marge Roukema (Rep.)
6th	Frank Pallone, Jr. (Dem.)

7th   Bob Franks (Rep.)
8th   Bill Martini (Rep.)
9th   Robert G. Torricelli (Dem.)
10th   Donald M. Payne (Dem.)
11th   Rodney P. Frelinghuysen (Rep.)
12th   Dick Zimmer (Rep.)
13th   Robert Menendez (Dem.)

NEW MEXICO

Senate

Jeff Bingaman (Dem.)
Pete V. Domenici (Rep.)

House

1st   Steven Schiff (Rep.)
2nd   Joe Skeen (Rep.)
3rd   Bill Richardson (Dem.)

NEW YORK

Senate

Alfonse D'Amato (Rep.)
Daniel Patrick Moynihan (Dem.)

House

1st   Michael P. Forbes (Rep.)
2nd   Rick Lazio (Rep.)
3rd   Peter T. King (Rep.)
4th   Daniel Frisa (Rep.)
5th   Gary L. Ackerman (Dem.)
6th   Floyd H. Flake (Dem.)
7th   Thomas J. Manton (Dem.)
8th   Jerrold Nadler (Dem.)

9th	Charles E. Schumer (Dem.)
10th	Edolphus Towns (Dem.)
11th	Major R. Owens (Dem.)
12th	Nydia M. Velazquez (Dem.)
13th	Susan Molinari (Rep.)
14th	Carolyn B. Maloney (Dem.)
15th	Charles B. Rangel (Dem.)
16th	Jose E. Serrano (Dem.)
17th	Eliot L. Engel (Dem.)
18th	Nita M. Lowey (Dem.)
19th	Sue W. Kelly (Rep.)
20th	Benjamin A. Gilman (Rep.)
21st	Michael R. McNulty (Dem.)
22nd	Gerald B. H. Solomon (Rep.)
23rd	Sherwood L. Boehlert (Rep.)
24th	John M. McHugh (Rep.)
25th	James T. Walsh (Rep.)
26th	Maurice D. Hinchey (Dem.)
27th	Bill Paxon (Rep.)
28th	Louise McIntosch-Slaughter (Dem.)
29th	John J. LaFalce (Dem.)
30th	Jack Quinn (Rep.)
31st	Amory Houghton (Rep.)

NORTH CAROLINA

Senate

Lauch Faircloth (Rep.)
Jesse A. Helms (Rep.)

House

1st	Eva Clayton (Dem.)
2nd	David Funderburk (Rep.)
3rd	Walter B. Jones, Jr. (Rep.)

4th	Frederick Kenneth Heineman (Rep.)
5th	Richard Burr (Rep.)
6th	Howard Coble (Rep.)
7th	Charlie Rose (Dem.)
8th	W. G. (Bill) Hefner (Dem.)
9th	Sue Myrick (Rep.)
10th	Cass Ballenger (Rep.)
11th	Charles H. Taylor (Rep.)
12th	Melvin L. Watt (Dem.)

NORTH DAKOTA

Senate

Kent Conrad (Dem.)
Byron L. Dorgan (Dem.)

House

At large: Earl Pomeroy (Dem.)

OHIO

Senate

Mike DeWine (Rep.)
John Glenn (Dem.)

House

1st	Steve Chabot (Rep.)
2nd	Rob Portman (Rep.)
3rd	Tony P. Hall (Dem.)
4th	Michael G. Oxley (Rep.)
5th	Paul E. Gillmor (Rep.)
6th	Frank A. Cremeans (Rep.)
7th	David L. Hobson (Rep.)
8th	John A. Boehner (Rep.)

9th	Marcy Kaptur (Dem.)
10th	Martin R. Hoke (Rep.)
11th	Louis Stokes (Dem.)
12th	John R. Kasich (Rep.)
13th	Sherrod Brown (Dem.)
14th	Thomas C. Sawyer (Dem.)
15th	Deborah Pryce (Rep.)
16th	Ralph Regula (Rep.)
17th	James A. Traficant, Jr. (Dem.)
18th	Bob Ney (Rep.)
19th	Steve C. LaTourette (Rep.)

OKLAHOMA

Senate

Jim Inhofe (Rep.)
Don Nickles (Rep.)

House

1st	Steve Largent (Rep.)
2nd	Tom Coburn (Rep.)
3rd	Bill K. Brewster (Dem.)
4th	J. C. Watts (Rep.)
5th	Ernest J. Istook, Jr. (Rep.)
6th	Frank D. Lucas (Rep.)

OREGON

Senate

Mark Hatfield (Rep.)
Bob Packwood (Rep.)

House

| 1st | Elizabeth Furse (Dem.) |

2nd   Wes Cooley (Rep.)
3rd   Ron Wyden (Dem.)
4th   Peter A. DeFazio (Dem.)
5th   Jim Bunn (Rep.)

PENNSYLVANIA

Senate

Rick Santorum (Rep.)
Arlen Specter (Rep.)

House

1st   Thomas M. Foglietta (Dem.)
2nd   Chaka Fattah (Dem.)
3rd   Robert A. Borski (Dem.)
4th   Ron Klink (Dem.)
5th   William F. Clinger, Jr. (Rep.)
6th   Tim Holden (Dem.)
7th   Curt Weldon (Rep.)
8th   James C. Greenwood (Rep.)
9th   Bud Shuster (Rep.)
10th   Joseph M. McDade (Rep.)
11th   Paul E. Kanjorski (Dem.)
12th   John P. Murtha (Dem.)
13th   John D. Fox (Rep.)
14th   William J. Coyne (Dem.)
15th   Paul McHale (Dem.)
16th   Robert S. Walker (Rep.)
17th   George W. Gekas (Rep.)
18th   Mike Doyle (Dem.)
19th   William F. Goodling (Rep.)
20th   Frank R. Mascara (Dem.)
21st   Phil English (Rep.)

RHODE ISLAND

Senate

John H. Chafee (Rep.)

Claiborne Pell (Dem.)

House

| 1st | Patrick J. Kennedy (Dem.) |
| 2nd | John Reed (Dem.) |

SOUTH CAROLINA

Senate

Ernest F. Hollings (Dem.)

Strom Thurmond (Rep.)

House

1st	Mark Sanford (Rep.)
2nd	Floyd Spence (Rep.)
3rd	Lindsey Graham (Rep.)
4th	Bob Inglis (Rep.)
5th	John M. Spratt, Jr. (Dem.)
6th	James E. Clyburn (Dem.)

SOUTH DAKOTA

Senate

Thomas A. Daschle (Dem.)

Larry Pressler (Rep.)

House

At large: Tim Johnson (Dem.)

TENNESSEE

Senate

Bill Frist (Rep.)
Fred Thompson (Rep.)

House

1st	James H. (Jimmy) Quillen (Rep.)
2nd	John J. Duncan, Jr. (Rep.)
3rd	Zach Wamp (Rep.)
4th	Van Hilleary (Rep.)
5th	Bob Clement (Rep.)
6th	Bart Gordon (Dem.)
7th	Ed Bryant (Dem.)
8th	John S. Tanner (Dem.)
9th	Harold E. Ford (Dem.)

TEXAS

Senate

Phil Gramm (Rep.)
Kay Bailey Hutchison (Rep.)

House

1st	Jim Chapman (Dem.)
2nd	Charles Wilson (Dem.)
3rd	Sam Johnson (Rep.)
4th	Ralph M. Hall (Dem.)
5th	John Bryant (Dem.)
6th	Joe Barton (Rep.)
7th	Bill Archer (Rep.)
8th	Jack Fields (Rep.)
9th	Steve Stockman (Rep.)

10th	Lloyd Doggett (Dem.)
11th	Chet Edwards (Dem.)
12th	Pete Geren (Dem.)
13th	William M. (Mac) Thornberry (Rep.)
14th	Greg Laughlin (Dem.)
15th	E. de la Garza (Dem.)
16th	Ronald D. Coleman (Dem.)
17th	Charles W. Stenholm (Dem.)
18th	Sheila Jackson Lee (Dem.)
19th	Larry Combest (Rep.)
20th	Henry B. Gonzalez (Dem.)
21st	Lamar S. Smith (Rep.)
22nd	Tom DeLay (Rep.)
23rd	Henry Bonilla (Rep.)
24th	Martin Frost (Dem.)
25th	Ken Bentsen (Dem.)
26th	Richard K. Armey (Rep.)
27th	Solomon P. Ortiz (Dem.)
28th	Frank Tejeda (Dem.)
29th	Gene Green (Dem.)
30th	Eddie Bernice Johnson (Dem.)

UTAH

Senate

Robert F. Bennett (Rep.)
Orrin G. Hatch (Rep.)

House

1st	James V. Hansen (Rep.)
2nd	Enid Greene Waldholtz (Rep.)
3rd	Bill Orton (Dem.)

VERMONT

Senate

James M. Jeffords (Rep.)
Patrick J. Leahy (Dem.)

House

At large: Bernard Sanders (Ind.)

VIRGINIA

Senate

Charles S. Robb (Dem.)
John W. Warner (Rep.)

House

1st	Herbert H. Bateman (Rep.)
2nd	Owen B. Pickett (Dem.)
3rd	Robert C. Scott (Dem.)
4th	Norman Sisisky (Dem.)
5th	L. F. Payne (Dem.)
6th	Bob Goodlatte (Rep.)
7th	Thomas J. Bliley (Rep.)
8th	James P. Moran (Dem.)
9th	Rick Boucher (Dem.)
10th	Frank R. Wolf (Rep.)
11th	Thomas M. Davis III (Rep.)

WASHINGTON

Senate

Slade Gorton (Rep.)
Patty Murray (Dem.)

House

1st	Rick White (Rep.)
2nd	Jack Metcalf (Rep.)
3rd	Linda Smith (Rep.)
4th	Doc Hastings (Rep.)
5th	George Nethercutt (Rep.)
6th	Norman D. Dicks (Dem.)
7th	Jim McDermott (Dem.)
8th	Jennifer Dunn (Rep.)
9th	Randy Tate (Rep.)

WEST VIRGINIA

Senate

Robert C. Byrd (Dem.)
John D. Rockefeller IV (Dem.)

House

1st	Alan B. Mollohan (Dem.)
2nd	Robert E. Wise, Jr. (Dem.)
3rd	Nick J. Rahall, Jr. (Dem.)

WISCONSIN

Senate

Russell D. Feingold (Dem.)
Herbert Kohl (Dem.)

House

1st	Mark W. Neumann (Rep.)
2nd	Scott L. Klug (Rep.)
3rd	Steve Gunderson (Rep.)

4th	Gerald D. Kleczka (Dem.)
5th	Thomas M. Barrett (Dem.)
6th	Thomas E. Petri (Rep.)
7th	David R. Obey (Dem.)
8th	Toby Roth (Rep.)
9th	F. James Sensenbrenner, Jr. (Rep.)

WYOMING

Senate

Craig Thomas (Rep.)
Alan K. Simpson (Rep.)

House

At large   Barbara Cubin (Rep.)

DELEGATES

American Samoa	Eni F. H. Faleomavaega (Dem.)
District Of Columbia	Eleanor Holmes Norton (Dem.)
Guam	Robert A. Underwood (Dem.)
Puerto Rico	Carlos A. Romero-Barcelo (Dem.)
Virgin Islands	Victor O. Frazer (Dem.)

INDEX